to

from

date

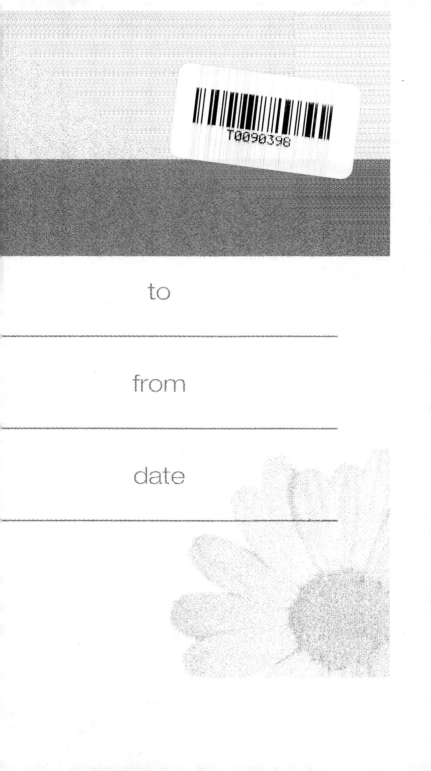

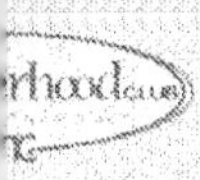

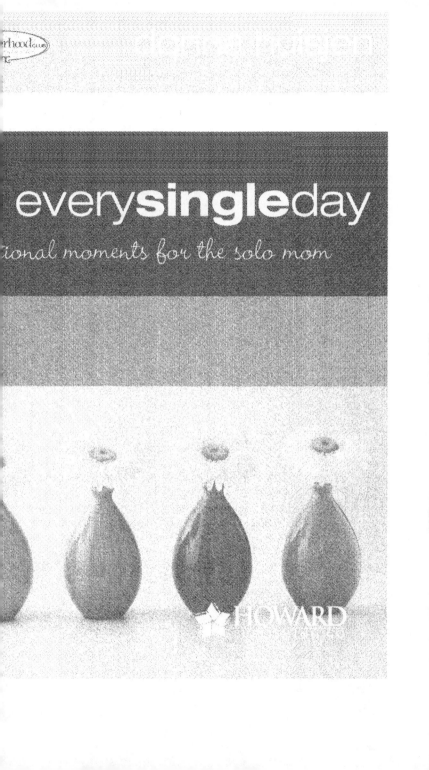

everysingleday

ional moments for the solo mom

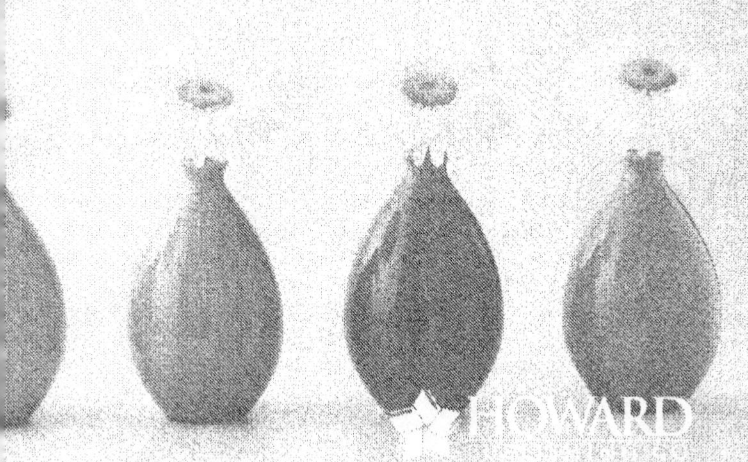

Our purpose at Howard Publishing is to:

- *increase faith* in the hearts of growing Christians
- *inspire holiness* in the lives of believers
- *instill hope* in the hearts of struggling people everywhe

Because He's coming again!

Published by Howard Publishing Co., Inc.
3117 North Seventh Street, West Monroe, LA 71291-2227
www.howardpublishing.com

06 07 08 09 10 11 12 13 14 15   10 9 8 7 6 5 4 3

Edited by Heather Gemmen and Mary Ann Jeffreys
Interior design by Stephanie D. Walker
Cover design by Diane Whisner

Library of Congress Cataloging-in-Publication Data
Husjein, Donna, 1951-
Every single day : devotional moments for the solo mom / Donna Huisje
p. cm.
ISBN 13: 978-1-4165-8317-2   ISBN 10: 1-4165-8317-3
1. Single mothers—Prayer-books and devotions—English. 2. Dev
calendars. I. Title.

BV4847.H87 2005
242'.6431—dc22

20050

"Will the Angels Let Me Play?" (1905) words by W. L. Werden; Music by F
Gladdish.

contents

contents

contents

contents

contents

introduction

If you've picked up this book, chances are, you and I share characteristics. First, *we're both moms.* This common identity our lives with color and vibrancy. Despite the stress, being a m one of the primary sources of our zest, our buoyancy, our resili Second, we both happen to be, for one reason or another, *go alone as parents.* This is not a commentary on our parenting a or success or even an implied negative. Based on your own per experiences with the "single" part of parenting, though, chance you can testify to additional pressures and complications that n working alongside supportive husbands might never experienc

Our children, circumstances, temperaments, backgrounds, outlooks vary as much as those of any moms. We get by with a or enjoy the advantages of a PhD, tread water to maintain a s living standard or float along with relative ease.

And the reasons for our singleness vary also. We range divorcées (with varying custody arrangements); to widows; to n married women who have entered motherhood through pregn adoption, guardianship, or foster-parenting; to single grandmot aunts, or sisters bearing shared or sole responsibility for chil And the list goes on.

My number one goal in this book is to relate to you as mo mom. I'll use observations and personal stories, both from my childhood and from my experiences as a mother and grandm Since I make no attempt to provide in these meditations a comp

introduction

re of me, I feel it only fair to explain myself briefly. I'm the adoptive mother of three grown daughters: Amanda (husband), Angela (ex-husband Walter), and Khristina. Walter has dy of his and Angie's three children: Walter Jr., Rebecca, and

ly experiences parenting three daughters, all adopted at older and carrying the scars of earlier trauma, will appear in snippets y connect to the topic at hand. Even when the particulars of necdotes and examples don't fit your circumstances exactly, hared-mom factor will bind us together and touch you at a ingful level.

ve provided a brief summary statement ("Take Away") at the of each weekday's meditation—something to carry with you ghout your day, possibly during those otherwise-idle moments you're sitting in traffic or waiting to pick up a child. The Saturday ial offers you an opportunity to "Wrap Up" the points you've and pondered during the week: an invitation to review the five Aways," a chance to "Tuck Away" an additional encouraging ture verse related to each of them, and a "Give Away" for each -a suggestion for how you might pass along insights from the to other single mothers with whom you might cross paths.

od bless you, Mom!

Mother's love is peace. It need not be acquired; it need not be deserved.

Erich Fromm

week 1

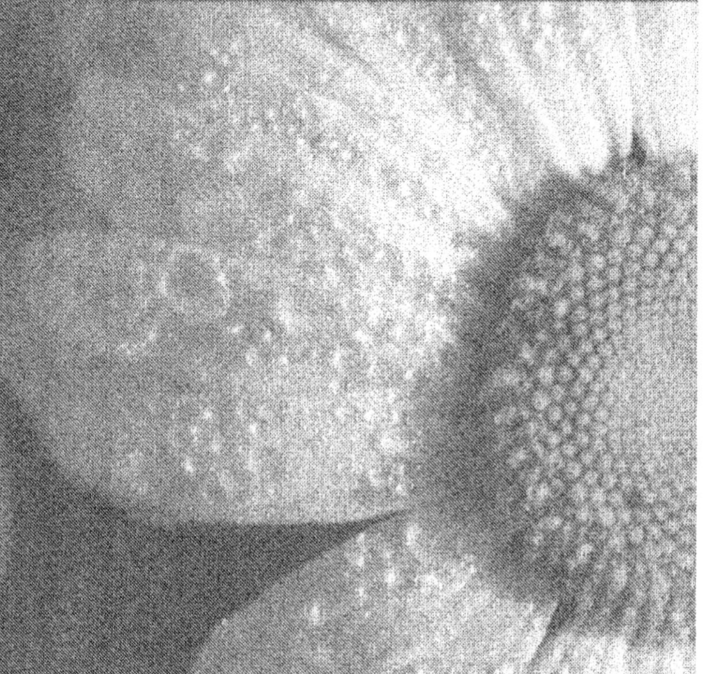

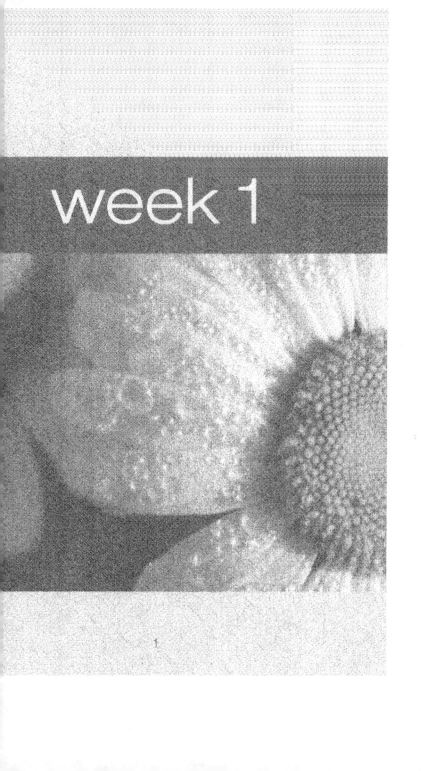

week 1

Enough

Do You Want to Know a Secret?

This is the day the LORD has made;
let us rejoice and be glad in it.
Psalm 118:24

When I was a teenager, my mom would occasionally purchase a chocolate bar—the kind with the bite-size rectangular portions- a Sunday-afternoon treat. The operative word here is *a*, as in *a* c bar—to be savored by a family of nine. I always tried to suck sl but found this taste teaser exasperating.

My life as a single mom at times reminds me of that choc chunk. My circumstances aren't always, or necessarily, bad, pleasures and feel-good times can seem few and short-lived. about you? Are you a chocoholic, someone who'd love to si savor (uninterrupted) a whole luscious bar? When a luxury or comes your way, would you prefer more than "just one"?

The apostle Paul was single, and his life was anything bu (check out 2 Corinthians 11:23–29). But Paul had, and sha life-changing secret: "I know what it is to be in need, and I what it is to have plenty. I have learned the secret of being cont nd every situation" (Philippians 4:12).

s we grow in grace, we learn to appreciate the little things of he satisfaction of a good soak and a great book as a day winds , the plash of a fish disturbing the surface of an otherwise l lake, the waft of a sudden breeze on a humid afternoon, a ssful shopping spree, the first crooked smile of an infant. "I believe I ate the whole thing" represents far less satisfaction than nexpected joy, following a simple pleasure, of "Life is sweet. a great sample I just got to taste!"

ly Provider, you pour out sweet moments and ous helpings of your goodness every day. Help rst to notice and then to savor them. Prevent me rating your gifts as small or large, and continue tch me unawares with your freebie surprises. Amen.

Take Away: I am content with God's minigraces.

week 1

Vicissitudes

God's Word for Your Day

Do not worry about tomorrow, for tomorrow will wo about itself. Each day has enough trouble of its ow
Matthew 6:34

"I need a word, Dad," I reminded. My ninth-grade teacher had us the assignment of coming to school each day equipped with a word to share. I accepted the challenge with enthusiasm, and never let me down. At the dinner table each evening I receiv addition to my cache, complete with an impromptu definitio been thirty-some years, but I still recall the first two nuggets gave me to broaden my verbal horizon: *facetious* and *geniality*.

Another word came as a bonus. Dad included this gem reg in his table prayers, and we kids figured out the definition fro context. *Vicissitudes* are circumstances, ups and downs, unfor challenges. They're all about change, uncertainty, vulnerability of control.

As a single mom your life is likely full of vicissitudes. I know is. Three daughters, a son-in-law, an ex-son-in-law with custody three grandchildren, financial concerns, fibromyalgia, a dema profession, and the physical needs of a house older than I—al

tuesday

toll. But even when life feels like a roller-coaster ride, when we ourselves lurching through the drama of every day, God gives capacity to enjoy the rolls and pitches, to close our tired eyes gh the tunnels, and to land on our feet, perhaps even ready for er go-around, at the end of the ride.

sus doesn't need to offer us a word for each day; *one word* from s enough for a lifetime! It's not a difficult word, either—you've n it most of your life, though its meaning deepens as you daily in wisdom: *sufficient*, as in "My grace is sufficient for you, for ower is made perfect in weakness" (2 Corinthians 12:9). God's and his love are sufficient—more than enough to meet and ome today's vicissitudes.

elp me, Father, to meet each vicissitude with a ous helping of your daily manna of grace. Allow maintain my sense of humor while basking in the y of your constant, loving presence. Amen.

ke Away: With God's help, I can overcome today's vicissitudes.

week 1

Pedigree

"Just Regular Human"

To all who received him, to those who believed in h name, he gave the right to become children of Goc children born not of natural descent, nor of humar decision or a husband's will, but born of God.

John 1:12–13

Several years ago my preadolescent adopted daughter annou with satisfaction to dinner guests that she was "half Indian." "' neat," was the polite response, "and what about the other ! Angie had already expressed the one distinction in which she the most pride, but if the question gave her pause, she quickly r ered, neatly packaging together every other aspect of her awak self-image: "Just regular human, I guess."

We humans enter the world equipped with an unc compulsion to niche ourselves. I, for instance, am a femal adult, a never-married, a mom, a grandma, a working woma optimist, an introvert, a right-brainer and right-hander, a "hav comparison to many), and an American.

Only one distinction, though, sets us apart in an ete meaningful way. We teach it to our children but then fail to reme ourselves: "If anybody asks you who you are, tell them you're a of God." In those times when you might feel alone—and even you deserve your isolation—remember that you're royalty, a ıter and adopted heir of the Creator-Father of the universe. Jesus, whatever your station or complicated state of life, you're a fide, pedigreed child of the King. As such, you can afford to ur head high as you go about your daily round of activity, just you.

ıd you're in an ideal position to pass along this assurance to "regular humans," like your kids. They may struggle to discover they are, but God's paternal commitment to them, and you, is ut restraint or condition.

ly Abba, you created me marvelously regular and called me to be irregular, extraordinary, special—yet ne exclusively. Your love knows neither bounds nor dance. I love you, Daddy! Amen.

ke Away: I'm royalty, a daughter of the King.

Anticipated but Unexpect

Your Will Be Done

Do not conform any longer to the pattern of this wo
but be transformed by the renewing of your mind. Th
you will be able to test and approve what God's will i
his good, pleasing and perfect will.
Romans 12:2

I had waited almost ten agonizing years for the adoption of a
ond child, and I wanted resolution. To impress God with my
cere impatience, I expressed myself emphatically: "I yearn. I cr
need. Get it, God?" But four hard-hitting words kept wallopin
"YOUR . . . WILL . . . BE . . . DONE!" Ouch! I could hear the
reverberate with each syllable.

Then God in his good will began to do a number on me. No th
to my own willpower, I began to mellow. I recognized that not
given another child might be "for my good" (my short definiti
God's intentions for me) rather than "for my own good" (that h
negative catchall I learned as a kid undergoing discipline). Iron
at that very point God acted. I awoke one morning unaccoun
excited, certain the awaited announcement would come so
was sharing my exhilaration with a coworker when the phone

thursday

rated at so mundane an intrusion, I forced my thoughts back a business track. I should have known: the caller was my social er, informing me that a nine-year-old was "waiting for me" to : her.

ver since then I've been able to view this long-awaited adoption s God's reluctant concession but as his slow—yet perfectly l—working out of his will. Despite my anticipation that day, urprise granting of my dream was somehow unexpected. And s for me a sure confirmation I have repeatedly grasped when vings might otherwise rock my shaky confidence. What "fluke" ssing or surprise timing of events has comforted you? Can you God's finger in it?

hank you, Father, that my circumstances aren't -nilly. With your help I can center myself, give up ruggle, and snuggle in the inner core of your will. those four wonderful words be my credo today and, al, my swan song: Your will be done. Amen.

Take Away: Trusting in God's will, instead of holding on to mine, brings blessings beyond imagination.

week 1

Teaching Compassion

Will the Angels Let Me Play?

Above all else, guard your heart,
for it is the wellspring of life.
Proverbs 4:23

When I was two years old, I had a favorite doll. This dolly was si cantly disabled (at some point her head had become detached her body and was now missing). My love for her was solidly on compassion.

I have another vivid, and seemingly connected, recolle from that age. It's about snuggling in my mother's lap, engr in a favorite song. Its lyrics would be considered maudlin by t standards: the child dies at the end. But the questions raised b chorus are indelibly etched in my memory:

Mama, when I go to heaven, will the angels let me play?
Just because I am a cripple, will they say I'm in the way?
Here the children never want me. I'm a bother, they all say.
Mama, when I go to heaven, will the angels let me play?

Chances are, you take your parenting seriously. You may your own, you tell yourself, but if you try hard enough, yo all the bases. You place appropriate emphasis on developing children's minds and bodies—but what about their hearts? In ompetitive society, kids jockey for position, concerned about standing in the social rankings. But the highest-ranking quality d's eyes is character. This includes the ability to empathize with s, to forego a measure of personal stature to lift someone else a higher.

ill your daughter team up with her wheelchair-bound classmate ess? Will your son stand up for the uncoordinated, hyper either team wants? If you're willing to show concern for the ess, headless dolls in your life, your kids stand a good chance of oping this capacity as well.

uthor of Compassion, teach me to care so that caring I may point my children in the way of ess. Amen.

Take Away: I can help my kids exercise their hearts.

Wrap It Up

Monday

Take Away

I am content with God's minigraces.

Tuck Away

God is able to make all grace abound to you, so that in all thi[ngs at] all times, having all that you need, you will abound in every [good] work. As it is written: "He has scattered abroad his gifts to the [poor"] (2 Corinthians 9:8–9)

Give Away

As I learn to revel in small blessings, I'll help someone else [who is] struggling to balance her ledger sheet of troubles and graces.

Tuesday

Take Away

With God's help, I can overcome today's vicissitudes.

Tuck Away

In this world you will have trouble. But take heart! I have overco[me the] world. (John 16:33)

e Away

n a friend shares her vicissitudes with me, I'll share with her the iency of Jesus.

dnesday

e Away

oyalty, a daughter of the King.

k Away

hing I ask of the LORD, this is what I seek: that I may dwell in the of the LORD all the days of my life, to gaze upon the beauty of the (Psalm 27:4)

e Away

ncreasingly assimilate the reality of my position with God, I'll others to understand theirs.

rsday

e Away

ng in God's will instead of holding on to mine brings blessings d imagination.

k Away

the LORD your God, who teaches you what is best for you, who directs you in the way you should go. (Isaiah 48:17)

Give Away

When I see God at work in my life, whether in real time or in spect, I'll share my excitement with someone else who may be ing for guidance.

Friday

Take Away

I can help my kids exercise their hearts.

Tuck Away

I will give you a new heart and put a new spirit in you; I w move from you your heart of stone and give you a heart of flesh. (E 36:26)

Give Away

I'll endeavor through example to interest others in the C centered aerobics of compassion.

notes

The moment a child is born, the mother
also born. She never existed before. Th
woman existed, but the mother, never. A
mother is something absolutely new.

Rajneesh

week 2

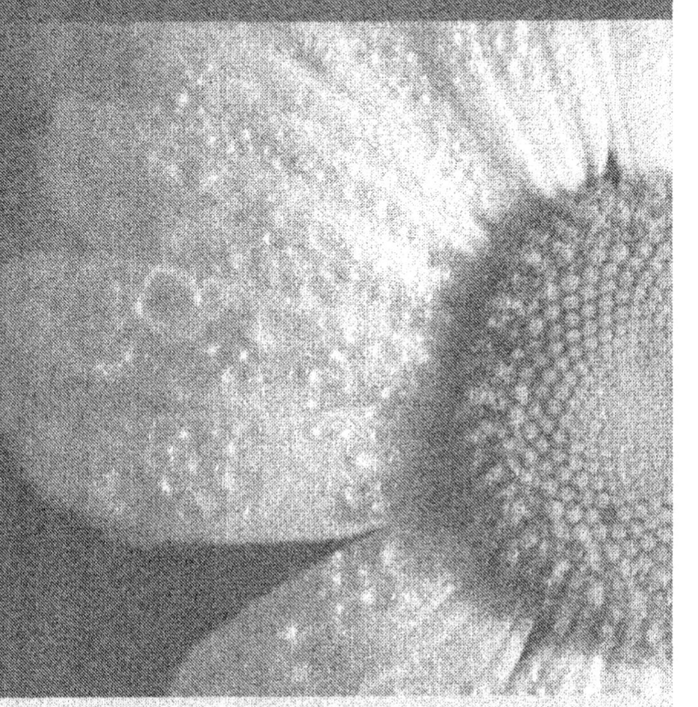

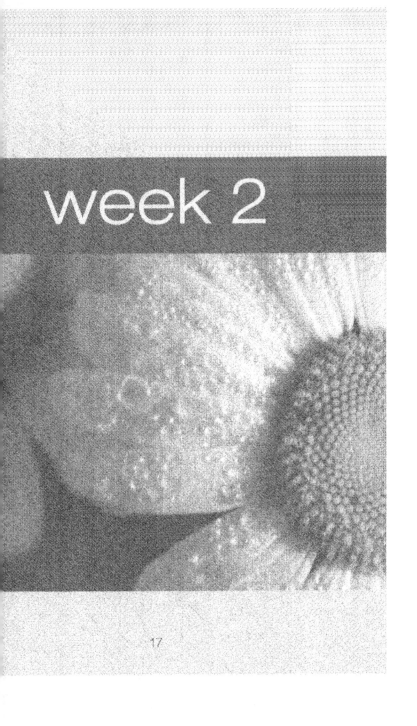

week 2

Henry

The Eternity Collection

God raised us up with Christ and seated us with hir
in the heavenly realms in Christ Jesus,
in order that in the coming ages he might show
the incomparable riches of his grace.
Ephesians 2:6–7

Henry, our newest family member, like Khristina, was seventee was ugly, Khris conceded, but his style suited her. He sported mal name tag, Cutlass Ciera. With his 33,700 miles, Henry w hoped) a bargain. In my sometimes impulsive fashion, I bough with an advance, backed by a plastic promise. Khris would reim me as she was able.

I've managed on my limited, single-parent income to send all of my daughters to Christian schools. It's been a worthwhile sac but a bigger issue has been the nature of the local Christian-s constituency. Most of Khris's high-school classmates were aff Henry didn't show well in the school lot. My teenage dau alternated between militant nonmaterialism and a desire for flight goods. Whenever she let slip sentiments like "I'm the p kid in school," I countered with, "But remember when we liv ıobile home?" This was shorthand for the indisputable truth: as the richest kid in our "park." Within the microcosm of that borhood, she enjoyed the best-dressed house (an attractive le-wide) of any of her peers.

atus is relative, and any attempt at an honest appraisal of ing demands the questions: *Compared to what?* or *Compared to* ? By the standards of two-thirds of the world, our household sperous beyond belief. But infinitely more important is our ing with God. As his children we already enjoy all the eternal he has to offer. Truth be told, our real treasure trove, the ity collection, places us in an absolutely out-of-this-world et. Do your kids know, really know, and appreciate the wealth possess in him?

hank you, Father, for the incomparable riches of your expressed in your kindness to me and mine in Jesus st. When I'm tempted to murmur, impress on my heart ard of relativity. Amen.

ke Away: I embrace the secret of relativity.

week 2

Looking Back

The Restoration Miracle

The Spirit helps us in our weakness. We do not kno
what we ought to pray, but the Spirit himself interce
for us with groans that words cannot express.
Romans 8:26

At eleven Angie developed a fixation with baby birds. It bega
spring afternoon when she and Khristina discovered a nest of "
doned" newborn sparrows. To my dismay, a pattern soon devel
For three consecutive springs I found occupied nests everywhe
cluding her underwear drawer. Always, the mother bird had
tragic end, and Angie, undeterred by previous failures, was rea
take over as foster mother.

Prior to joining our family (her second adoption), Angie had
kicked out of the nest repeatedly, and she felt a need, her the
explained, to reenact her autobiography in an attempt to make t
turn out differently. "See, Mom," she sighed one windy eveni
route to a therapy session. "The poor birds can hardly fly. It m
scary looking back at where they've already been!"

Both Angie and Khrissy specialized during those first ye
adoption in cryptic, coded messages. Angie's poignant com

have been nothing more than an observation, but her tone raway look alerted me that she was in memory mode. My heart for her, and I breathed a silent prayer for her eventual healing. any single moms are haunted and constricted by painful ories and shattered dreams. The wonder is that God knows y where you've been, where you are now, and where you're d. You may not ask for, expect, or feel yourself worthy of his g touch. But behind the scenes, even when you're too numb, sted, or cynical to pray, his articulate Spirit is at work, pleading cause. And then one day, when you find the courage for ight, you'll be caught off guard by the miracle of restoration appened when you weren't even looking.

oly Spirit, help! The words have flown from my Catch, parse, and arrange them—then direct them e shortest path to the Father's heart. Amen.

ke Away: The Spirit is pleading my cause.

week 2

Walking Wounded

Bitterness: The Poisoned Soul

The word of God is living and active.
Sharper than any double-edged sword, it penetrat
even to dividing soul and spirit, joints and marrow
it judges the thoughts and attitudes of the heart.
Hebrews 4:12

Several summers ago Khristina participated in a missions t Honduras to construct homes for hurricane victims. While wo she accidentally jumped on a metal peg protruding from the crete. It penetrated her shoe and entered her arch, requiring gency treatment and three days on crutches. Fifteen months lat ankle and foot began to swell, resulting in an abscess and we treatment by a podiatrist. Stumped, he finally opted for explo surgery. The result was "one for the books": the Honduran h personnel had left a small, round piece of tennis-shoe insole foot, resulting in a stubborn infection that had climbed the sheath into her ankle.

When have you unwittingly allowed a "foreign object, resentment, to fester in your soul, possibly for a long time?

a nasty wound to impale your spirit and implant it there in rst place—an injury that may have contributed to your current ness. You found yourself betrayed, acutely wounded. But you ged somehow to forge ahead, seemingly unimpaired, priding elf on your resilience.

ventually, though, when a wound hasn't properly healed, thing can trigger a relapse. A virulent infection begins to spread gh your soul, swelling into putrid, full-blown bitterness. At this you need surgery. Your poisoned spirit requires infiltration by alpel of God's convicting Word. The Master Surgeon follows gh with the intravenous antibiotic of his love until you're pain- ontagion-free—restored to go about the business of living with ved buoyancy in your step.

ne Bible is as relevant today as any therapeutic approach; its cine is timeless. Why not allow the Great Physician to examine reat your ailing soul?

reator, Healer, I've been wounded. Purify my soul the salve of your love. Restore and free me, I pray. en.

ake Away: My Soul Surgeon urges me to make and keep regular appointments.

week 2

Supplemental Income

God's Provision for Rest

Come to me, all you who are weary and burdenec
and I will give you rest.
Matthew 11:28

When I was in elementary school, my dad, a fireman who wc twenty-four-hour shifts with days off in between, found innov ways to augment our family's single income. For a period of he set tile, saving enough odds and ends from various jobs tc a "collage" shower to our family bathroom. After he became inspector, an elderly lady bequeathed to him an authentic spir wheel from her attic. Using it as a model, Dad designed, built sold door-to-door a number of working replicas.

Many single moms are also single-income moms, and it's a tr worth repeating that creativity is born of necessity. For th years Amanda, my oldest, and I were alone, I babysat regularly took in a succession of female boarders, much to the delight c outgoing daughter. In recent years I've enjoyed writing and free editing. If you're involved with a second job—a paper route, clo alterations, crafts, envelope stuffing, wedding coordination, ıs, or house-sitting—you are among the ranks of those using ingenuity to coax those elusive ends to meet.

ıt one vital element of life too easily becomes expendable at the ic pace this secondary employment requires—rest. Jesus knew nportance of physical, spiritual, and emotional restoration. e carved out time for it, both for himself and for his disciples. ıe accepted interruptions graciously, but we can presume his tion deficit was eventually made up.

om the beginning God instituted a Sabbath rest for his creation, ıo extenuating circumstances exempt you from the unwind he's built into the rhythm of life. Got a minute? An hour? A y you can plump? It's great supplemental income for your body, , and spirit.

…aah! I'm tired, Jesus—drifting off to sleep. …ks for assuring me that you never sleep on the job, …ing me the much-needed time "off task" that you … for your children. Amen.

…e Away: Proper rest is a worthwhile priority.

week 2

Hazards

Potholes and Speed Bumps

Have no fear of sudden disaster or of the ruin that
overtakes the wicked, for the LORD will be your confide
and will keep your foot from being snared.
Proverbs 3:25–26

Potholes regularly pockmark our town in early spring, but lately opposite have been sprouting up, with annoying regularity, the shortcut routes I prefer for my daily commute. Whether e around or over them, I'm equally frustrated by potholes and bumps.

Speed bumps are invasive—planned, planted, and perma They're not, on the whole, dangerous, and they do serve a pur they're strategically placed in the roadway for the express gc getting cars to slow down.

The pothole, on the other hand, is truly haphazard, and its d is quite real, especially when camouflaged by snow or water. particular pothole is at first encounter altogether unexpected. U the rounded, uniform mound that covers the roadway and in every driver, the ragged pothole seems to claim arbitrary casu Life's pothole encounters tend to be, or feel, catastrophic—wh e crises that jolt us suddenly or losses that occur with terrifying unstoppable slowness: tragedies like death, divorce, custody tes, job loss, or serious illness.

fe's speed-bump intrusions may provoke us to complain over demands for us to slow down. But life's pothole victim—too an already struggling single mom with minimal support—may gainst injustice in general or God in particular.

r, pothole casualties don't have to cause spiritual fatalities. In they can have the opposite effect. Have you noticed that an nulation of minor frustrations can slowly draw you away from while a single disaster can drive you straight into his arms? good has come from a pothole encounter in your life?

Dear Lord, please slow me down regularly with life's bumps, but stop me in my tracks with the occasional le. Amen.

ake Away: I can find God in and through devastating circumstances.

week 2

Wrap It Up

Monday

Take Away

I embrace the secret of relativity.

Tuck Away

How priceless is your unfailing love! (Psalm 36:7)

Give Away

I'll help my discouraged friend to view her situation against the drop of God's dependable love.

Tuesday

Take Away

The Spirit is pleading my cause.

Tuck Away

My witness is in heaven; my advocate is on high. My intercessor friend as my eyes pour out tears to God. (Job 16:19–20)

Give Away

Prompted by the Spirit's gentle nudges, I'll help to instill inspi and expectation into another's despondent heart.

dnesday

e Away

oul Surgeon urges me to make and keep regular appoint-
s.

k Away

rful heart is good medicine, but a crushed spirit dries up the bones.
erbs 17:22)

e Away

I observe in a friend the telltale signs of festering resentment,
artily recommend my Great Physician.

rsday

e Away

r rest is a worthwhile priority.

k Away

entance and rest is your salvation, in quietness and trust is your
th. (Isaiah 30:15)

e Away

vite a friend to share a restful outing or other refreshing
ience.

Friday

Take Away

I can find God in and through devastating circumstances.

Tuck Away

God is our refuge and strength, an ever-present help in trouble. The… we will not fear. (Psalm 46:1–2)

Give Away

As I become more adept at locating and experiencing God in t… times, I'll mentor another hurting mom in the dynamics of ide… ing his hand.

notes

Mother love is the fuel that enables a
normal human being to do the impossib

Marion C. Garretty

week 3

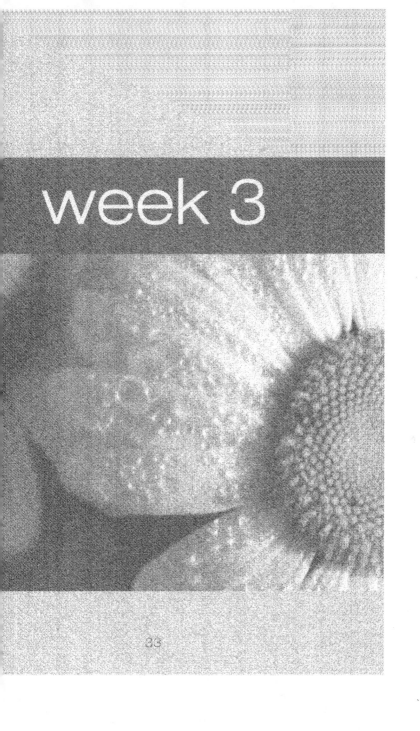

week 3

Signs

When God's Will Isn't . . .

Why are you downcast, O my soul? Why so disturb
within me? Put your hope in God, for I will yet praise
Psalm 42:5

Years ago a single coworker with two daughters gave up her jo house to marry a father of seven she had known only briefly. W two weeks it became clear that he wanted only the free service homemaker/caregiver. Through decisive action she arranged to the marriage annulled, her position reinstated, and the sale home canceled.

"Too good to be true" situations can be exactly that! The explode in our faces, leaving the sad confetti of shredded d to drift to the ground around us. The scenario might be th of a second marriage or of a promising relationship. Some moms, like my friend, are good not only at adapting to chang also at adopting new loved ones in the plural—including nev and extended family. In my friend's particular situation, the br involved not only being wrenched apart from the man she th she loved but having to watch helplessly as her own children su the shattering loss of would-be family members.

emarriage and family blending may be God's plan for you, now
er. But if you feel yourself hurtling into a relationship headlong
eadstrong, be wary. It's easy to misread events as signs of God's
g, particularly if you're in a hurry. But big-picture hindsight
llows you to see his will may be available only further down
th.

metimes God shows us what his will *isn't*. Unexpected or
ple obstacles may trip us up, or we may struggle with a sense
omething isn't right. Has it ever seemed as though God were
g you away from something you badly wanted? Take heart: he
s and desires only the best for you—and he'll let you know if,
en, he wants you to move ahead!

*laker, Matchmaker, Peacemaker, make me receptive
ur will and open to your comfort. Open my eyes;
me see, now or later, the rightness of your plan for
Amen.*

ake Away: My impulses don't necessarily correspond to God's will.

week 3

Junctions

Control on the Slope

The mind of sinful [people] is death, but the mind controlled by the Spirit is life and peace.
Romans 8:6

I was surprised to hear recently that "speed may have been a [p cutable] factor" in a tragic skiing collision on a Colorado Nonskier that I am, my initial reaction was along the lines of you tell someone hurtling down a mountain to hurtle slower? response to an inquiry enlightened me: Larger, busier ski slopes intersections and stringent traffic rules in place. A person is sponsible to exercise control on a pair of skis as behind the wh a car.

When you find yourself plunging toward the pit of de propelled by the gravity of your circumstances and chased avalanche of regret, you're still responsible to exercise self-contr obey rules. Not simply of human decency, but of God. Each your path crisscrosses someone else's, you make a deliberate dec Regardless of your route or the condition of the slope, yo react with hostility or respond in the Spirit with courtesy and natively, you can hole up in the lodge, avoiding altogether affic of life. It's in this mode that we become distant parents, ilable friends, dispirited warm bodies staring blankly into fires red and anger.)

ivorce, separation, or other adverse circumstances may have ed your run. You've been injured—or lost your nerve, sense of g, or feel for the snow. Maybe you feel angry, rash, uncaring. ttacking the slope like a loose cannon will only endanger you thers and alienate the very ones you want to have on your team. u rejoin life's disciplined circuit, guided and controlled by the , you'll regain courtesy, composure, and peace.

Holy Spirit, attend me on my straightaways and in my alls, but be especially near at my junctions. Grant e strength to obey the law of love and avoid collision es. Amen.

Take Away: God's law of love is my foolproof guide.

Durable Sandals

Thanking God for Nonproblems

Do not worry, saying, "What shall we eat?" or "Wha
shall we drink?" or "What shall we wear?" For . . . yo
heavenly Father knows that you need [these things
Matthew 6:31–32

Have you ever encountered the astounding claim in Deutero 29:5: "During the forty years that I led you through the desert, clothes did not wear out, nor did the sandals on your feet" ancient Israelites must have had an efficient hand-me-down sy in place. But ultimately, as his people marched, drifted, or s their course, God saw fit to protect their feet from the searing sands.

As a mom going it alone, you may at some point have encouraged by the statistic that 80 percent of your worries will materialize. But even if this elusive percentage could be verified, about the infinite number of *potential* pitfalls you never even th to worry about? What about your son's bike, flung carelessly o lawn, that *didn't* disappear? Your one child in three whose tee perfectly aligned? The potentially serious close call in traffic you too preoccupied even to notice? How often do you take the ti

. God for the blessing of averted danger, for the nonproblems ould have become major concerns?

y ex-son-in-law, Walter, has picked up two catch phrases from a ack friend, six words he's internalized to the point that they've d his outlook on life: "Life happens" and "It could be worse." Life nly does happen, to each of us—but so does grace. Otherwise, situation would be unimaginably more difficult than it is today. provides strength to deal with whatever problems you face, but o protects and prevents. He showers you with blessings you'll even know about, and he keeps a high percentage of nagging ifs from moving beyond that category.

my Provider, help me to trace your hand in the s of my day and to perceive your staying hand in the ents that might have been catastrophic. Amen.

Take Away: I thank God for the problem-free areas of my life.

Connecting

Father to the Fatherless

The LORD your God carried you, as a father carries his
all the way you went until you reached this place.
Deuteronomy 1:31

Khristina, assigned by her Christian elementary-school te the task of memorizing the Ten Commandments, balked a fifth. Unable from her literalist viewpoint to honor both fathe mother, when it was obvious to all that she had only one of th uisite parents, she took is upon herself to make a neat substitu "Honor your holy Father and your mother." Unwittingly, Kl was expressing a leap of faith we desire from all our kids, wh or not an earthly dad is in the picture.

How we go about instilling within our children a healthy n of God as Father is a question much debated; we live in days dysfunctional relationships are almost normative. In Psalm David makes an interesting claim: God takes upon himself th of Father, specifically when an earthly dad is absent. He is "a to the fatherless."

If "Daddy" hasn't been in the picture for your kids, or i

e hasn't been pretty, they'll see no point in connecting with a nly Father. In fact, they may avoid him, particularly if they're of harsh discipline. If you want them to overcome this hurdle, first order of business will be to make sure your own Father daughter relationship is intact. Only then can you show (and hem what your heavenly Abba means to you.

oth the pastors in my church are gentle fathers who relate well to ngregation's youngest members and delight all of us with their tful and interactive children's sermons. On a recent Sunday ing Walter Jr. sat with his Auntie Khris and me in the back row seating bay. Neither Khris nor I had suspected Walter's take e pastoral role. "Pick me up," he insisted in a strident whisper. 't see God!"

his is your daughter, God, touching base for laily chat. Thanks for giving me your undivided tion and for taking me seriously, even when I le. Teach my kids to feel as comfortable with you do. Amen.

Take Away: My task is to persistently strive to lead my kids to God.

Winter's End

Teasers of God's Grace

The God of all grace, who called you to his eternal glory in Christ, after you have suffered a little while, will himself restore you.
1 Peter 5:10

If you live in a climate characterized by bleak and seemingly i minable winters, you'll relate to the near-epidemic occurren spring fever on that first unseasonably warm, mid-March da invariably struck by the frenetic degree of outdoor activity. (couples walk briskly, still encased in sensible coats and heac Short-sleeved homeowners relish the opportunity to tackle u ished leaf raking. Clumps of bike-riding kids, whose parents a lenient frame of mind, sport bare feet and T-shirts. Dogs c with excitement as they strain against their leashes. Everywher look you observe sun-starved neighbors furiously luxuriating i still chilly rays.

Your wintry season may have been private. Maybe you experi death, divorce, separation, unanticipated pregnancy, reloc job loss, financial reversal, or some other trauma. But gra days begin to lengthen; you emerge from your hibernation, ning off your gray weariness. As you take your first tentative you, too, experience days and hours when the sun once sometimes unaccountably, shines for you. Surprised by ism, you let down your guard enough to conceive of a small ment—perhaps a project, visit, or outing—that might not too much to hope for.

fore spring gains a foothold in west Michigan, my feet will slip on ice. My grandchildren's eager shoes will experimentally ut snow, slush, puddles, and mud. Warmth may come gradually he result of a sudden change in wind direction, but it will one ttle in to stay. If you're experiencing a winter of discontent astation, why not look ahead to those God-given foretastes ter days to come, those heavenly teasers of the fullness of his

hank you, Father, for the unaccustomed warmth y cheek, the spring in my step, and the bubble of joy bugging me today. Amen.

Take Away: God's warmth penetrates and thaws my spirit.

Wrap It Up

Monday

Take Away

My impulses don't necessarily correspond to God's will.

Tuck Away

I am always with you; you hold me by my right hand. You gui[de me] with your counsel, and afterward you will take me into glory. ([Psalm] 73:23–24)

Give Away

When I observe a friend on the verge of a rash decision, I'll [share] what I've learned—and the One I know!

Tuesday

Take Away

God's law of love is my foolproof guide.

Tuck Away

God is love. Whoever lives in love lives in God, and God in [her]. (1 [John] 4:16)

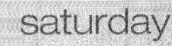

e Away

oach the subject gently when I see a friend struggling with ictive impulses.

dnesday

e Away

ık God for the problem-free areas of my life.

k Away

ORD will keep you from all harm—he will watch over your life; the will watch over your coming and going both now and forevermore. n 121:7)

e Away

ceive with grace and thankfully recite for my hurting friend the ngs I might otherwise have overlooked.

ırsday

e Away

ısk is to persistently strive to lead my kids to God.

k Away

ather has compassion on his children, so the LORD has compassion se who fear him. . . . From everlasting to everlasting the LORD's love is with those who fear him, and his righteousness with their chi[...] children. (Psalm 103:13, 17)

Give Away

The better I get to know my heavenly Father, the more effecti[...] will be able to introduce him to others.

Friday

Take Away

God's warmth penetrates and thaws my spirit.

Tuck Away

See! The winter is past; the rains are over and gone. Flowers appear [...] earth; the season of singing has come. (Song of Songs 2:11–12)

Give Away

As I seek to relate to my friend in her gloom, I'll carry the Son[...] with me.

notes

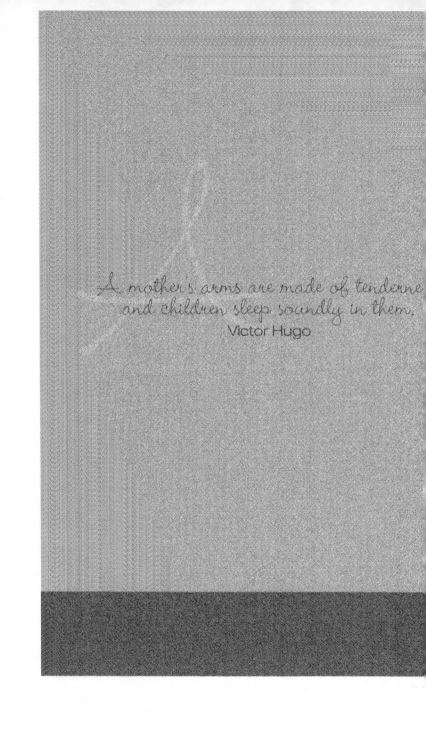

A mother's arms are made of tenderne
and children sleep soundly in them.

Victor Hugo

week 4

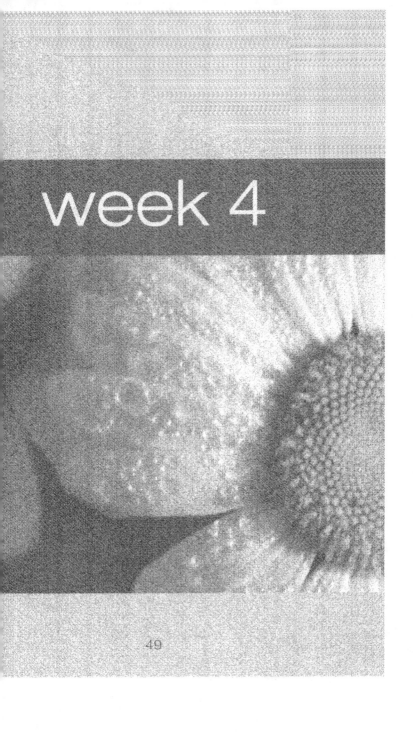

Consolation

Songs in the Night

I thought about the former days, the years of long
I remembered my songs in the night.
Psalm 77:5–6

When I was eleven, my mom passed away of cancer, leaving m to parent five young children. One bright spot in those afte days drew me forward like a beacon signaling hope. During M illness Dad had received a record album by a male chorus, fea songs of comfort.

And comfort they were! Nightly, at bedtime, Dad would ov the stillness with the mellow strains of classic Christian music. from old-fashioned hymns of consolation became best friends, company I ritually savored night after night. The music punct the dreary routine of those early days of loss with thrilling exclan points of anticipation.

You may prefer piano concertos, string quartets (Psalm reminds Israel's king that "the music of the strings makes you g praise choruses, the intricate harmonies of an a cappella gro Southern Gospel favorites. Or, if you're oriented more vi fort food" for thought—perhaps a nightly helping from the of Psalms—may better prepare your mind and heart for the tion to sleep.

may be that the daytime hours seem tolerable to you but that ng stretches of darkness—devoid of diversion, demands, or ship—drone on interminably. Forced to face stark realities, n't deny your loneliness and pain. Your kids have battled this ime oppression too. Have you thought of introducing the of Bible reading, story, or song and prayer to draw all of you he Father's embrace during those critical minutes (or hours) sleep? If you're wrapped in his protecting arms, nighttime can best time, for all of you.

hanks, Father, for the songs you've given me to my nights special, even intimate. Help me in the ess to listen for and hear your voice of consolation guidance. Amen.

ake Away: God's embrace sweetens the darkness for my family and me.

week 4

Slippage

God's Way or Leeway?

Watch yourselves closely so that you do not forget
things your eyes have seen or let them slip from yc
heart as long as you live. Teach them to your childr

Deuteronomy 4:9

Ever observe your toddler immediately acknowledging a b rule with that high-mileage exclamation "uh-oh"? An inkli morality has dawned (or at least an association made betwe tion and predictable consequence). But the self-control neec prevent the behavior in the first place hasn't yet kicked in.

Evasive tactics and transparent lying follow soon enough, a willful preschooler becomes more sophisticated. By the time little one has reached school age, though, she should be equ with a working conscience that requires only gentle but firm dir to ensure that it engages under the proper circumstances.

Remember the first time your teenage self broke with a pa taboo? At first you felt the pinch of an internal "uh-oh." But after a your oh-so-adult ability to rationalize soothed your ruffled consc You were perfectly content with your adjusted standard for norm

Do you ever feel that the frustrations of single mothering

o some slack? The issue may involve anger management, age usage, driving habits, or indiscriminate dating practices. e you've started sleeping in on Sunday mornings, smoking nking in front of your kids after acknowledging the health ls, or watching sexually explicit sitcoms in their hearing. To pressionable seven-year-old, such actions can be alarming. hild is left to sift through a dilemma: either his standard e issue or his mom must be wrong, and he'll be reluctant to inate Mom.

e reality is, if you want your kids to follow Jesus, you do well odel consistent, Christlike behavior. Your own—and their— ced spiritual health, along with your revitalized relationship he Savior, will be worth the effort.

h-oh! I've blown it again, God. My best intentions lipped right through my fingers. Please forgive d help my children find the grace to do the same. n.

e Away: My children need to see consistent Christlike behavior in me.

week 4

Hotdogs with Our Buns

Your Father knows what you need before you ask h
Matthew 6:8

Years ago a single coworker with three small children quipped receiving a minimal pay raise, "Now we can have hotdogs wit buns!" A good line, yes, but poignant, nonetheless, for the deg reality it represented.

David's statement in Psalm 37:25 may raise your eyebro have never seen the righteous forsaken or their children be bread." *Come on, David!* you want to protest. *Never? How ca have missed the hollow faces on the streets of downtown Jeru* Like the principles in Proverbs, David's words reflect typical universal—reality. Yet they still offer comfort; God didn't ir them in his Word, after all, to mislead you.

How often have you stayed awake at night, brow furrowe a budget gridlock? Will $50 per week purchase sufficient groc $40? How long a grace period do you have for that credit-car When is the next five-payday month? Did you forget that money for next semester is due next week?

Ever think of asking the Holy Spirit to deflect your thought

cash-flow issues toward praising "God from whom all blessings
" Then put away your calculator (or squelch the mental math),
ver, and trust him to refresh you with sleep. He has the budget
y worked out—and he guarantees not to forsake you (Joshua
Seek first the things of God, and the stuff of this life (hotdogs
ilk money included) will come to you as well (Matthew 6:33).
me God who restores you with sleep (Psalm 127:2) will never
provide for your other needs.

hank you, Father, that I can approach you, not as gar, but as your beloved, even pampered, daughter. y, my cup overflows! Amen.

Take Away: God will meet all my needs.

week 4

Support

I Told You So!

A friend loves at all times,
and a brother is born for adversity.
Proverbs 17:17

I told you so! These four short words, sounding in our imagin: like hammer blows, can cause us as single moms to withdrav fail to seek the support systems we crave. Sadly, our own hear be our most vocal critics, so the company inside our retreat is l more pleasant than that "out there."

You may be an unwed mother, separated, divorced, wid married to an incarcerated or AWOL husband, starting ove single grandma with custody of grandkids, or an adoptive mom possibilities go on and on. Regardless of the details, real or ima disapproval can prevent you from seeking assistance you really

It may be that your critics have faded into the past, but pride holds you back from hinting at a need. Or you may from those who, never having expressed criticism at all, seem above your level of trial and error. You may visualize fellow c members or acquaintances as "beautiful people" with lives c of problems. Maybe you even expect your kids to help carry le that your lives are just as "together" as theirs.

rhaps the secondhand casualties of your earlier pain (parents, gs, former friends) still treat you icily. Maybe it's a matter of ation (yours and, by extension, theirs). Or a memory of endless (theirs) that seemed to fall on deaf ears (yours) and caused less arguments (yours in the plural). But chances are, others ried to chip away at the ice encasing your heart. If you'd allow an audience, you might be surprised to hear "I wanted to help. *to tell you so.*"

u love me, Lord, no matter what, and you're ys there for me. I know because you tell me again again—in your Word and in my heart. Open me up se people you delegate to encourage and include me. n.

ke Away: Others want to give me support.

week 4

Facsimile

The Image of Dad

You knit me together in my mother's womb.
I praise you because I am fearfully and wonderfully m
Psalm 139:13–14

The adoptive records of one of my daughters reveal that sh pushed away by her birth mother at two years of age becaus reminded her of an older daughter who had died.

Admirers are quick to examine a newborn's ph characteristics and early personality indicators, happily verba their considered opinions: "He's the *image* of his daddy. She h mommy's eyes . . . Grandma's chin . . . Mom's temper . . ." (the genetic miracle of new life, such an exercise is natural an a puzzle that doting family members are eager to solve.

But the child who reminds you of his absent father may you. His appearance, habits, or gestures may anger you the w dad's did. Without your even realizing it, your emotions, whic be quite appropriate for dad, are transferred to son. Or her cha smile and extroverted personality may elicit a longing for th who has abandoned you. Caught up in the preoccupation moment, you unintentionally blame your little girl for failing erson you want to see when you look into her eyes.

dly, a child will perceive and *accept* rejection from an early age. see such a pattern taking shape, it's vital that you ask the Holy for the grace to forgive. Not to forgive your son for being o his genetic makeup, but the man who injured or deserted -and ultimately yourself for allowing the pain to trickle down ır precious little one.

ɔd cherishes each of us for the one-of-a-kind creations we Our individual fingerprints reveal swirls and brushstrokes so ctive that they set us apart from all other people. We are, each l, individual, unique image bearers of God.

hank you, Sculptor, for the nimble touch of your tips in fashioning every aspect of me—and of my . Help me to see in this little one not a reminder of one I loathe or miss but a cherished, eternal facsimile ou. Amen.

Take Away: My kids are unique and precious individuals.

Wrap It Up

Monday

Take Away

God's embrace sweetens the darkness for my family and me.

Tuck Away

On my bed I remember you; I think of you through the watches night. Because you are my help, I sing in the shadow of your (Psalm 63:6–7)

Give Away

Aided by my sensitivity to the particular perils of nightfall, I'l my friend find nighttime serenity.

Tuesday

Take Away

My children need to see consistent Christlike behavior in me.

Tuck Away

The secret things belong to the LORD our God, but the things re belong to us and to our children forever, that we may follow all the of this law. (Deuteronomy 29:29)

e Away

the Spirit's help, I'll model my heart commitment for my kids, intances, and neighbors.

dnesday

e Away

vill meet all my needs.

k Away

n you rise early and stay up late, toiling for food to eat—for [God] sleep to those he loves. (Psalm 127:2)

Away

ge my friend to focus on one potential "deficit" within her l—time spent at rest. God will stay up and attend to everyelse.

rsday

e Away

s want to give me support.

: Away

is open rebuke than hidden love. Wounds from a friend can be . (Proverbs 27:5–6)

Give Away

If someone is shoring me up, I'll pass along that strength to ot

Friday

Take Away

My kids are unique and precious individuals.

Tuck Away

The LORD has chosen you to be his treasured possession. (Deutero
14:2)

Give Away

I'll encourage other single moms to cherish the individuality o
own children.

notes

A little girl, asked where her home wa[s,]
replied, "Where mother is."

Keith L. Brooks

week 5

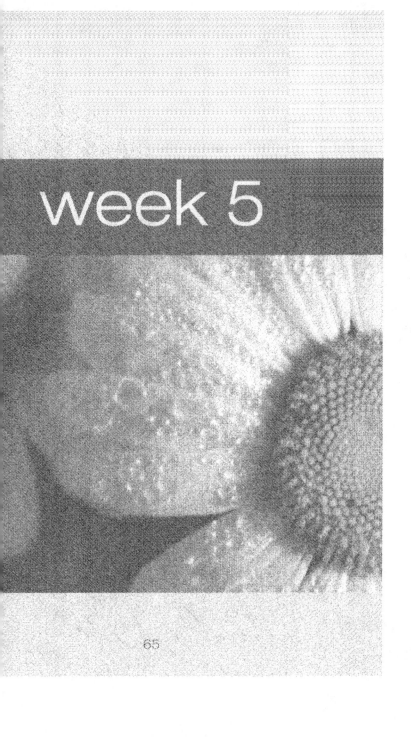

Security

A Better Home

How priceless is your unfailing love! Both high and low find refuge in the shadow of your wings.
Psalm 36:7

When Khristina was seven, we visited her older birth sister had recently been adopted into a well-to-do family. En route Khrissy observed in characteristic bluntness, "Jennifer got a home than I did." With sinking heart I probed for details. To Kl I should have known how she came to this conclusion: our n home shook during the washer's spin cycle!

A few years ago Khris resisted our moving from the mobile into a house, mourning particularly her huge climbing tree. Wi my knowledge she took souvenirs: a key, the chain from a ceilin a switch plate.

Both Angie and Khris had been adopted earlier into af families, but neither had difficulty adjusting after the disru of their earlier placements to our more modest lifestyle. Angi eleven: "I like the nice warm house my mom provides for me. I I was too much trouble in my other homes. But that's not a pr anymore because I've got a home where people love me." Khr

ven: "This is a littler house than I'm used to, but it's more
tant to be loved."

littler house, but a better home! You may worry about whether
umble living quarters you provide measure up to the more lavish
s of your kids' dad, relatives, or friends. But a limited income
't limit love, and you might be surprised to discover your kids'
m in identifying ultimate values.

e psalmist David observed, "Even the sparrow has found a
. . . where she may have her young—a place near your altar"
84:3). Ah, herein lies the critical point. Is your home not only
nd warm but "near God's altar"? If so, you're providing a nest
kids will remember as a haven of security.

*elp me, Lord, to provide for my children a secure
near your altar. May our snug nest overflow
that one priceless commodity: love. Amen.*

ke Away: My words and actions show my kids the value of love.

Moving On

Leave No One Behind

When I said, "My foot is slipping," your love, O LORD
supported me. When anxiety was great within me
your consolation brought joy to my soul.
Psalm 94:18–19

"Leave no one behind" has for years been a motto of the armed of the United States. Countless servicemen have risked their li reentering a battle zone to ensure that no comrade—trappe jured, or killed—has been abandoned.

When my mom passed away, she was survived by five children, two of whom were emotionally "left behind" for a as the family moved on. Rick, at ten, had difficulty succes negotiating the stages of grief. He was to become, for a whil displaced—even "misplaced"—child. Rick found it bewilderi relate to our new mother when she took over the mom funct year later. Terri, at five, slipped into a kind of shock, from whi didn't fully emerge for almost two years.

Death, separation, or divorce is a family experience. It's inev that individual members, depending upon age, dispositio circumstances, will respond or react in unique ways. One chil ıt; another may regress. One may behave perfectly, another vithdraw, and still another may take on the role of man of the .

you're the abandoned mom (figuratively or literally), you may ence a degree of devastation that leaves you close to debilitation. ıay find yourself able to function on the surface but incapable ıning to the nuances of need in each individual child.

critical, though, that no one be lost permanently as the family s to move on. At some point you need to "count noses." If you or another of your kids are lagging behind, it's time to seek ention. Most importantly, you'll want to kneel with the hurting and together seek the consolation God is waiting to give.

ly family's been stopped in its tracks, Lord, but y one we're shaking off our torpor and beginning to on. Teach us to hold hands and look both ways as enter the flow of life. Don't allow us to suffer a lly. Amen.

ke Away: My kids and I can move forward together after a crisis.

week 5

Transmitting Faith

Moms in the Making

These commandments that I give you today are to
upon your hearts. Impress them on your children. T
about them when you sit at home and when you w
along the road, when you lie down and when you ge

Deuteronomy 6:6–7

It's amazing how quickly little girls pick up mothering skills. my granddaughter, Rebecca, was twenty-one months old, she nated between bullying nine-month-old Tavis and smotherin with kisses and hugs, turning his smiles to alarmed surprise squeezed too enthusiastically. But I perceived her emerging m ing skills most clearly when her little brother was lured by my litter box: more often than not, when Becky observed the destir of his crawling beeline, she clattered after him, calling in ge concern, "No, no, 'Ahvees. No, no!"

Toddlers love to mimic. The fact is that our daughters an of all ages observe and imitate our parenting techniques mor we sometimes realize. If they have no younger siblings, you ones will practice with dolls, stuffed animals, and even pets small. As they grow, their treatment of other children and will reflect the attitudes and even platitudes they've learned at knees.

a solo mom you may be ultraconscious of your modeling some areas. But how high on your priority list is passing ur faith? It's easy to allow exhaustion to excuse you from an devotional life, but you do your kids a disservice if you expect is to take over in this critical area. You can't fake faith. Or itment. Your kids will know. They pick up on the degree of ation between your faith and your life, probably more than alize. "Remember your leaders [might we say *moms*?], who the word of God to you," counsels the author of Hebrews. ider the outcome of their way of life and imitate their faith" ews 13:7).

elp me, Father, to impress upon my kids the love modeled for me. Mold and enfold them in the way, so that one day they'll pick up with my children where I've left off. Amen.

Take Away: If I love and serve God sincerely, my kids will notice.

Discovery

The God Who Will Be Found

I love those who love me,
and those who seek me find me.
Proverbs 8:17

Have you ever watched a toddler playing hide and seek? He'll s impatiently in his hiding place and will soon jump out, sque "Here I am!" It's as though the suspense is beyond his ability t If you pretend momentarily not to see or hear him, he'll run t in triumph, exhilarated at having been found.

First Chronicles 28:9 and 2 Chronicles 15:2 use identical p ology: "If you seek him [God], he will be found by you.' Jeremiah 29:13–14 personalizes the concept: "'You will seek n find me when you seek me with all your heart. I will be fou you,' declares the LORD." Notice that God neither promises to out your hiding place nor assures you that you'll eventually u his. No, God *wills* himself to be discovered by you.

In the case of the delinquent Israelites, God went further still. 65:1 makes an amazing claim: "I revealed myself to those who d ask for me; I was found by those who did not seek me. To a natic did not call on my name, I said, 'Here am I, here am I.'"

u may consider some aspects of what brought you to single :hood off-limits to anyone else—including God. You may even : of your way to avoid his searching eye. He might seek you out onfront you, or his modus operandi may be to wait for your But you may be sure he'll never deliberately remain beyond each. Instead, he'll plant himself on your path, calling "Here I .ike your gleeful little one, he longs to receive and reciprocate :mbrace.

'ank you, Lord, for not leaving me to grope my through life a frustrated seeker. Help me to readily ıd to your coaxing and coaching, plotting my :e in response to the direction of your "Here I am." n.

Take Away: God wants me to seek and find him.

week 5

Solace

Refuge in His Arms

The eternal God is your refuge,
and underneath are the everlasting arms.
Deuteronomy 33:27

My daughter Amanda suffers from neurological, perceptual, and cal impairments. Her disabilities aren't always immediately ob her disarming smile and articulate verbal skills may camouflag deficits for a while. She exudes a level of confidence hinting at l ability and functionality than she can at times muster. Now m for several years, she and Doug are happy according to their own dards. As an outgoing and sensitive—but not necessarily percep child and adolescent, though, Amanda had trouble reading social Unfortunately, she had no problem interpreting the taunts, p and outright torment she endured from other kids.

When the skirt of her new jumper was ripped by fourth- boys, I carefully stitched the jagged tear, but I was powerless to the wound when a high-school classmate called as a joke her on a date. Later we would work together on coping skill immediately afterward we entered a cocoon together, welcoming o join us. Amanda fondly recalls my singing old hymns with till today she and I openly discuss the hurts of her childhood. er gratitude toward me and unconditional acceptance of others ily remarkable.

hen your kids are teased about circumstances over which they no control (like their dad's character or absence), you don't need embarrassed or inhibited about comforting them with words of invite God to uphold you both as you seek to offer consolation. ronomy 33:27, on the previous page, is an amazingly powerful If you can somehow convey to your sons and daughters, in ver language is comfortable to you, the solace God is waiting ord, you'll give them a salve to see them all the way through this d into the next.

ounselor, keep me from awkwardness as I seek ssure my kids of your love. Don't let them dub it nfort and take it to mean dishonesty. Console and them, Holy Spirit, when they hurt. Amen.

e Away: God joins in as an active participant as I seek to comfort a hurting child.

Wrap It Up

Monday

Take Away

My words and actions show my kids the value of love.

Tuck Away

Better a meal of vegetables where there is love than a fattened cal hatred. (Proverbs 15:17)

Give Away

Rather than expending time and money for a fancy feast to ent an isolated mom and her kids, I'll focus on making them feel fortable and welcome in my home.

Tuesday

Take Away

My kids and I can move forward together after a crisis.

Tuck Away

Your Father in heaven is not willing that any of these little ones be lost. (Matthew 18:14)

e Away

on the lookout for floundering friends and acquaintances in ons similar to my own: an ounce of perception can unleash a prevention.

dnesday

e Away

ve and serve God sincerely, my kids will notice.

k Away

show you my faith by what I do. (James 2:18)

e Away

id the occasional wave, I'll reach out to that single mom two down.

rsday

e Away

vants me to seek and find him.

k Away

you seek the LORD your God, you will find him if you look for him ll your heart and with all your soul. (Deuteronomy 4:29)

Give Away

I commit to sharing with my friend the treasure God has wille
to find.

Friday

Take Away

God joins in as an active participant as I seek to comfort a hı
child.

Tuck Away

As a [mother] has compassion on [her] children, so the LORD has co sion on those who fear him; for he knows how we are formed, he re bers that we are dust. (Psalm 103:13–14)

Give Away

With a tweak or two in my approach, I'll share the same co
with my friend that I have shared with my wounded child.

notes

Youth fades; love droops;
the leaves of friendship fall;
a mother's secret hope outlives them all.

Oliver Wendell Holmes

week 6

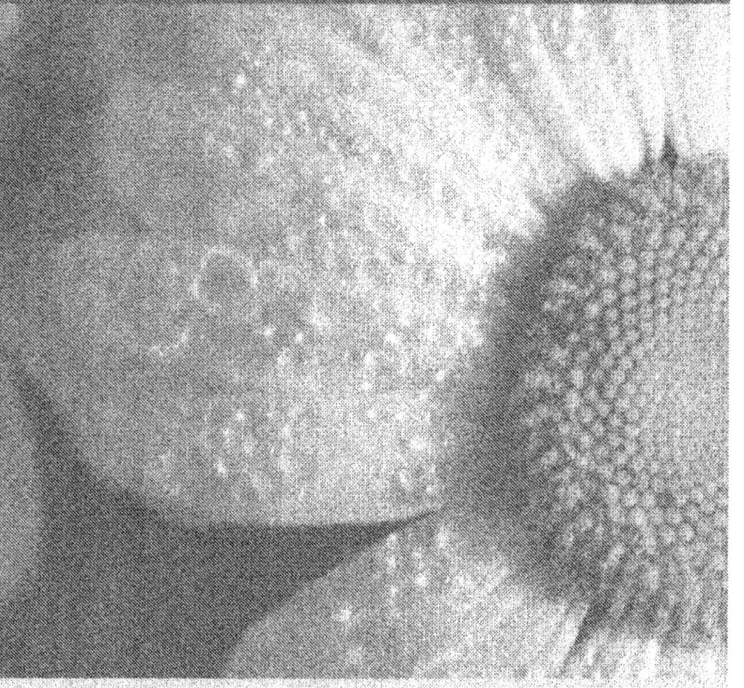

week 6

Covering

Spreading His Protection over The

Let all who take refuge in you be glad; let them ever for joy. Spread your protection over them, that those love your name may rejoice in you.

Psalm 5:11

My grandson Tavis experienced the first year of his life, along both his parents, in my home. During this time his two olde lings, both toddlers, spent a little more than a year in foster But Angie, struggling with emotional issues, found the dema motherhood beyond her coping ability, and she and Walt are n vorced. Eventually, Walt and the three children moved to thei home.

For a night or two after they had all left, I found myself m a nightly bedtime ritual. My final activity before retiring to my had been to check on Tavis to make certain he was adequately co I enjoyed spreading a blanket over him. Although he would ne aware of my loving gesture, I pictured him awakening duri night, surprised by the comfort.

You try in many ways to spread protection over your Depending upon their ages and stages, this may take the fo ay gates, caps and mittens, safety procedures, television rules, ıet guidelines, or curfews. Sometimes it may be necessary for le-custodial mom to equip the school with strict guidelines as o is authorized to pick up her child. As you send your kids on way each morning, you're turning them loose in a dangerous ometimes even predatory world. At the moment of goodbye, se an element of control.

at this point that Psalm 5:11 ("Spread your protection over) can bring tremendous comfort. *You* may relinquish control rarily, but you're turning it over to their, and your, personal tor. Each of you is enveloped, snug and secure, in the center care.

e door has slammed, Lord, and my kids are again from my sheltering care and influence. Wrap all day in an embrace wider than mine; spread your ctive net over each of them. Amen.

ke Away: God watches over my kids when they're separated from me.

week 6

Mutual Admiration

God's Delight in You

The LORD . . . will take great delight in you, he will quiet
with his love, he will rejoice over you with singing.
Zephaniah 3:17

This verse presents a memorable portrait of a parent soothing a with a lullaby. The nerve-jangling "waaahs" gradually subsi sniffles, which succumb to shudders. Finally, the tear-streake breaks into a sunny smile as parent and child engage in mutu miration. For the time being, the infant is bathed in delight.

The prophet Zephaniah wasn't talking only about babies. B intimate analogy of God/child, here applied to God/city (Jerus can meaningfully be carried over to God/daughter—you or m

How often do you picture God *delighting* in you? Tole yes. Forgiving, certainly. Your theology would be seriously if you didn't believe that God forgives. But do you think to your baby once you've been able to distract her from tears? Yo breathe a sigh of relief, but you find her toothless grins and g irresistible, don't you? Forgiving her, let alone begrudging her fussiness, is the farthest thing from your mind.

When you're overstressed, overtired, and overwhelmed

nmon adjectives for a mom going it alone), it's easy for you to to God as a longsuffering father making yet another allowance u. But how much more fulfilling your relationship could be if ould recognize the pure pleasure God derives from his bond you. You may approach him with eyes red from shame or g, but when he gazes at you, he sees the face of a beautiful and d daughter. God treasures your moments of quality Father/ ter time. Like a colicky infant, you may again need him to he floor with you. But for the time being, he takes exquisite re in your company.

l times I've craved your tolerance, God; when er, I've dared to ask your forgiveness. Your delight ond my limited imagination. Please help me to ecate your loving absorption in me. Amen.

Take Away: My doting Father God delights in me.

week 6

Weightless Freedom

Soaring to the Heights

Our light and momentary troubles are achieving for u
eternal glory that far outweighs them all.
2 Corinthians 4:17

"Light and momentary troubles?" Not mine! I've been div widowed, abandoned, betrayed, dumped, cheated on (you fill blank). From where I'm standing (or lying, here in the dark problems feel like a constricting weight on my chest, and I foresee resolution any time soon.

But think about the troubles Paul had in mind when he wro verse. His litany of harrowing experiences (check out 2 Corin 11:23–28) is more impressive than any list you or I could dred

It seems strange, though, for Paul to describe *glory* in ter weight. My notion of heaven recalls pictures of the weightlessne seen in television documentaries about astronauts who've risen the pull of Earth's gravity. The closest you've probably come sensation is when you were underwater, where you found yc as a child able to leap and somersault without the restriction generally govern your range of movement.

It may be helpful to think of old-fashioned scales, a set of pa erbalance each other. The substantial weight of God's promised will one day tip the scales to such a degree that you (on the side with your pack of worries) will find yourself soaring to agined heights.

avid used the word *scale* in another sense after God had delivered rom the weight of enemy oppression: "With my God I can a wall" (Psalm 18:29). What a beautiful analogy of weightless om! And David didn't have to wait for heaven to make this nent. Your problems may not seem momentary, but neither are ever-ending. Nor is the eternal glory Paul spoke about merely neday" proposition. Look around you. What glimpses of glory your eye right now? Eternity, after all, started a long time ago.

e grown accustomed, Lord, to lifting and dragging weights. Substitute, I pray, your infinitely more ntial weight of glory. Then teach me the gymnastics of om. Amen.

ake Away: I can enjoy glimpses of God's glory today and assurance of the fullness of that glory to come.

Embedded in the Conflict?

Peace I leave with you; my peace I give you. I do n
give to you as the world gives. Do not let your hearts
troubled and do not be afraid.
John 14:27

The twenty-first century has carried armed combat to a
unimagined only a few years ago. Like a macabre sporting
the war in Iraq during its initial phase became something
armchair-spectator affair. You, like the reporters who provide
time documentary coverage, may have felt yourself, for bet
worse, embedded in the conflict.

Despite patriotic stirrings, many of us recognize a deg
complexity and contradiction in the Iraqi conflict that
disturb us in the same way just a decade earlier in the firs
war. Unaccustomed to so high a degree of negative interna
sentiment, we Americans may tend to take this personally,
ourselves hated, to blush and cringe when we hear of anti-Am
protests.

At whatever point you became a single mother, you no
experienced a degree of fear of the unknown. But is fear of the

arily more desirable? At what point does sensory overload eract the benefits of live-action coverage? Where do we find elicate balance between TMI (too much information) and IIB ance is bliss!)?

e emotional backlash of catastrophic events like war and ism can invade the well-being of the isolated and mistreated. single mom you may find during tense periods that already ar emotions—fear, loneliness, alienation, demoralization, (warranted or otherwise)—are heightened. You may feel elf under a cloud of despair or restlessness. It may seem that the n that would, under "normal" circumstances, not have been f your life has seeped uninvited into a mind and heart already owded with stressors.

such times you do well to remember that God is closer still. pirit is *embedded within you*, offering you for the asking the and security this world and your nation can never give.

mbed yourself within my heart, Holy Spirit, till stlessness is gone. Entrench your peace so deep me that fear, alienation, and shame can find no to root. Amen.

Take Away: I live securely in the peace Jesus affords.

Adaptation

That's right!

You are a chosen people . . . a people belonging to C
that you may declare the praises of him who called y
out of darkness into his wonderful light.
1 Peter 2:9

Years ago my then two-year-old nephew, perplexed at followi extra-wide mobile home for miles along a two-lane highway, blurted out, "That's not right!" A moving house no more fit hi of reality than a cow jumping over the moon.

Grandson Walter Jr., who entered the foster-care syste eighteen months old, readjusted quickly, at thirty-four mont life with the daddy he adores. Despite the kindness of his parents, Walter J. never expressed doubt about who he was whom he belonged. He bravely bided his time until life once conformed to the pattern he knew to be "right."

As months went by, the foster-care worker suspected tha determined little boy was deliberately choosing—a protest of s to limit his use of spoken language. His long-awaited retu Daddy abruptly ended Walter J.'s long silence. Walt (Dad) me in triumph one morning soon after the reunification ommunicator" had picked up a cup and observed matter-of- "Look. There's water in here."

ildren need to bond and belong, and they have an uncanny from an early age to know the difference between genuine nd mere kindness or toleration. As family structures bend and —even when daddies exit the scene or custody is shared—kids apt with identities intact so long as they sense that they're truly and precious.

ddlers readily accept, too, that they belong to Jesus—who cherishes, and watches over them. When they internalize this from their days of earliest awareness, they'll have little reason r years to question the "rightness" of their faith.

elp me to instill within my little ones an absolute ition of the rightness of their love for you, Lord. t be so intrinsic to their self-awareness that it forms sis for their budding identities. Amen.

ke Away: Both God and I treasure my kids.

week 6

Wrap It Up

Monday

Take Away

God watches over my kids when they're separated from me.

Tuck Away

[God] will cover you with his feathers, and under his wings you wi
refuge. (Psalm 91:4)

Give Away

I'll invite my friend to slip under the security blanket Go
spread for my family.

Tuesday

Take Away

My doting Father God delights in me.

Tuck Away

[The LORD] brought me out into a spacious place; he rescued me b
he delighted in me. (2 Samuel 22:20)

Give Away

I will look at single moms as women God delights in and int

to God by showing them His love.

dnesday

e Away

enjoy glimpses of God's glory today and assurance of the full-f that glory to come.

k Away

vereign LORD is my strength; he makes my feet like the feet of a e enables me to go on the heights. (Habakkuk 3:19)

Away

repare to meander on the heights of God's love. I'll nudge my oor to be my strolling buddy.

rsday

e Away

ecurely in the peace Jesus affords.

k Away

ill be secure, because there is hope. You will lie down, with no one e you afraid. (Job 11:18, 19)

Away

re the Good News with that acquaintance who is struggling to manage, day by day, without a source of hope.

Friday

Take Away

Both God and I treasure my kids.

Tuck Away

How great is the love the Father has lavished on us, that we sho called children of God! (1 John 3:1)

Give Away

I'll share a genuine love with my dispirited friend and help her s "rightness" of being in God's family.

notes

It's not easy being a mother.
If it were easy, fathers would do it.

From the TV show *The Golden Girls*

week 7

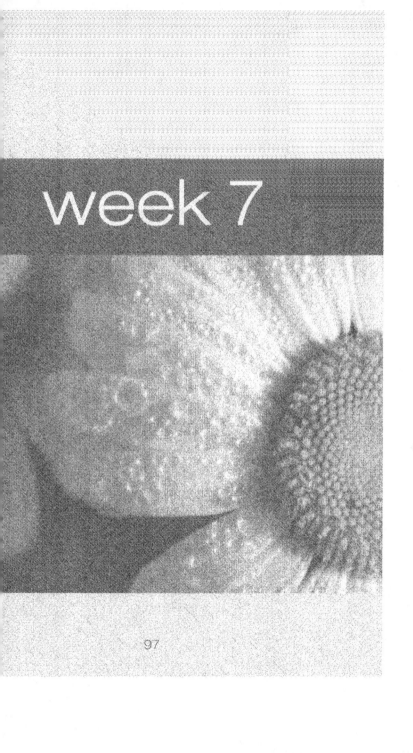

Edification

Beware of Falling Words!

The LORD was with Samuel as he grew up, and he l
none of his words fall to the ground.
1 Samuel 3:19

What exactly does it mean for words to fall to the ground? I u
stand the acoustic implication of mumbling the lyrics of a son
the pages of a hymnal. And you can muffle your speech by try
connect with your toes instead of with another human being
the author of 1 Samuel 3:19 seems to be describing words li
would a piece of fruit falling from a tree and decaying in the d

First Samuel 2:26 provides another summary of the
Samuel's growth pattern: "The boy Samuel continued to gr
stature and in favor with the LORD and with men." Hmm. S
a lot like another familiar verse: "Jesus grew in wisdom and st
and in favor with God and men" (Luke 2:52).

I suspect that Samuel chose his words carefully. When we,
other hand, feel entitled by the frustrations of single mothe
to nag our kids, grouse about our situations, gossip, insinu
otherwise run at the mouth, our words might as well fall
ground.

e apostle Paul sometimes used two *e* words with regard to
: *edification* and *encouragement*. If we'd keep them in mind,
ect we'd open our mouths less often and our words would fall
r to the ground nor on deaf ears. Whether your audience is
child or another family member, a friend, coworker, fellow
h member, or stranger, you, too, will grow in wisdom, spiritual
e, and favor with God and those around you if you limit your
to the worthwhile. If your words do have value, be sure to
t them outward, toward others who may benefit from what
ave to say.

*afi my words, Lord, so they may lift up my
s. Blow them upward and outward; keep them
t till they've accomplished a good purpose for you.
n.*

Take Away: My words can support and encourage those around me.

week 7

Truth

As for Me and My Household

If serving the LORD seems undesirable to you, then choose for yourselves this day whom you will serve. But as for me and my household, we will serve the L

Joshua 24:15

You know all too well that you can't speak *for* your kids, at lea those in that 'tween dimension flanked by middle school and pendence. Reading the first part of Joshua 24:15, I hear myse dressing Khristina, who in her late high-school years spouted consistent with our times. Life choices are too often laid out our kids on a buffet table. Some are more exotic than others, tend to be presented as valid and defensible.

Khris read her Bible but challenged my insistence that Christ is essentially different from other religions. For that matter, that phase she disliked the word *religion* and even *faith*. I heard sounding alarmingly lame in my confrontations (er, discussions her. I *did* face her, though, with my personal version of the fir of this verse: *If the Christian faith disagrees with you, or you u then find something else. But either way, decide.*

You can't force compliance with the rest of this verse, bu

eclare your home a God-honoring zone. Many kids from parent households are subjected to opposing influences and les from their other parent. But opposite, or even different, t necessarily equate to equal. Christianity's claims are simply gotiable. It's up to us to establish and maintain minimum ırds of faith compliance while our kids are under our roofs.

ur defiant or questioning adolescent may be waiting for you to t that. In this confusing world with so few absolutes, your kids uncompromising, clear-cut truth—and the example of a mom dvocates and *lives* for it. Youthful distrust may be a smoke for a burning desire for the *real* (a word kids do like). You and possess that elusive entity. Don't be reluctant to share.

elp me, Spirit, to lift high for my household the ard of faith. Work within the impressionable minds kids, so they may step up when my arms ache from g the banner alone. Amen.

Take Away: I declare my home a God-honoring zone.

week 7

Celibacy

Standing Up under Temptation

No temptation has seized you except what is comm
to [people]. And God is faithful; he will not let you b
tempted beyond what you can bear. But when
you are tempted, he will also provide a way out
so that you can stand up under it.

1 Corinthians 10:13

We live in a noncelibate world. At least that's the message dru
into our heads, subtly or overtly. You may feel deprived, o
touch, even odd, if you choose not to engage in sexual activity.

Some of you might feel particularly vulnerable on weekends
the kids are at their dad's. You're counseled to look out for n
one (yourself, of course). The implication is that you took s
place all week and deserve gratification as you recharge on yo
days. After all, who's to know or care?

The unavoidable reality is that God does both—intimatel
deeply. David in Psalm 139 specifies that God knows whe
sit, lie down, or stand. Verse 5 sounds like a protest: "You he
in, behind and before; you have laid your hand upon me." "
Preach it, David!" the rebel in you might want to shout.

ıt wait! David's next words catch us off guard: "Such knowledge wonderful for me." The psalmist relished his knowledge of attentiveness. David wasn't concerned about what he could ay with while God's back was turned but about the comfort of ng that nothing could snatch him from God's care. Check out words on this theme in Romans 8:38–39.

rnication and adultery are against God's law and will for us ad only to trouble and regret. Your Father understands your or refreshment, and he provides all the rejuvenation you need gh his Word and Spirit. If sexual enticement is an issue in your onfront God about it. He created you, complete with your and cravings, and he's able and eager to see you through.

ly Designer, you created me like yourself—complex ree. But with these qualities come the options of Thanks for calibrating me so carefully that you exactly how much stress I can withstand—and for ng me when I approach my limit. Amen.

ake Away: I can resist sexual temptation.

week 7

Christ's Power

From Strength to Weakness—and Ba

He said to me, "My grace is sufficient for you, for m
power is made perfect in weakness." Therefore I w
boast all the more gladly about my weaknesses,
so that Christ's power may rest on me.
2 Corinthians 12:9

Until several years ago I lived in a body so healthy I sometimes v myself as invincible. This superwoman self-image led me to se maintain high standards for personal accomplishment. But i kept me feeling alienated from those fortunate souls around m "had needs" and "deserved" relaxation and attention.

One morning, during a round-table discussion at an o meeting, I found myself so overwhelmed by fatigue that I co keep my eyes open, let alone focused. This was followed by rec bouts of weakness and pain, affecting much of my body. Two later I learned that I had fibromyalgia and chronic fatigue synd Despite the need for rest and pacing to spread a thin layer of e over a frequently too-long day, I'm managing.

"Becoming human" was a relief for me, but I've learnec vulnerability has its down sides too. You may know this

. Many single moms suffer from stress-related and/or chronic
ats and conditions, from migraines to depression to multiple
is to cancer. Factoring such stumbling blocks into the list of
s you face daily as you lurch around life's racetrack can make
exhausting and demoralizing existence. After all, you're trying
intain momentum, speed, balance, and equilibrium, all while
ating regular obstacles.

ul's perspective on this issue is refreshing. Only a God *identified*
would stoop to perfect his power through interaction with your
ess. How typical of the gospel's topsy-turvy messages in which
t are first and the meek are heiresses! The God who delights in
finds joy in shoring you up, lifting you in his everlasting arms
life's racetrack, and depositing you gently—just across today's
line.

*ven Christ, your grace is infinitely more than
ale for my needs, and my weakness only serves to
e and showcase your power. Thank you! Amen.*

ke Away: God perfects his power through
interaction with my weakness.

week 7

Generosity

Giving from an Unfilled Storehous

"Test me in this," says the LORD Almighty, "and see if not throw open the floodgates of heaven and pour o much blessing that you will not have room enough fc

Malachi 3:10

I don't believe that God in this verse is inviting us to test h Gideon did with his fleece (Judges 6:36–40) or Thomas wi probing fingers (John 20:24–29). He's offering a conditional ise, contingent upon our willingness to trust and obey him matter of Christian giving.

This issue can be problematic for a single, overstretched struggling along on a single, overstretched income. You may heard that if you take your gift to God off the top on payday, have enough left over for remaining obligations. And the Bibl seem to teach this. But if this were a magic formula, the w money markets would have caught on long ago. The reality the math doesn't always work out so smoothly; there may ev times when you're obliged to swallow your pride and approa church for help with a pressing, unmet need.

Paul states: "If the willingness is there, the gift is acce

ling to what one has, not according to what [she] does not have. the present time your plenty will supply what [others] need, so n turn their plenty will supply what you need" (2 Corinthians 14). Paul encourages generous giving when you can (and a ous attitude all the time); he also gives permission to make your known when *others are able.*

od's tantalizing promise, voiced through Malachi, stands not entive but as reassurance of the boundless supply of blessing aiting to cascade on you. When God invites you to test his you may feel free to do so. He's not about to let you prove rong!

e seen those floodgates open, my Provider, over over, exactly when I needed your blessing. Help me st you enough to hold loosely to what you've given refrain from preoccupying myself with tomorrow's Amen.

Take Away: Generosity is mine to give and to receive.

week 7

Wrap It Up

Monday

Take Away

My words can support and encourage those around me.

Tuck Away

Pleasant words are a honeycomb, sweet to the soul and healing *bones.* (Proverbs 16:24)

Give Away

When my friend feels "down in the mouth," I'll attempt to lift h with words of encouragement.

Tuesday

Take Away

I declare my home a God-honoring zone.

Tuck Away

Choose life, so that you and your children may live and that you m the LORD your God, listen to his voice, and hold fast to him. For the is your life. (Deuteronomy 30:19–20)

e Away

ay that others may sense the aura of God's presence in my home they visit.

dnesday

e Away

resist sexual temptation.

k Away

not have a high priest who is unable to sympathize with our weak- but we have one who has been tempted in every way, just as we et was without sin. (Hebrews 4:15)

Away

discuss this sensitive issue with other unattached moms, I'll them in the direction of a far more satisfying connection.

rsday

e Away

erfects his power through interaction with my weakness.

k Away

he one you love is sick. (John 11:3)

Give Away

I'll point my friend away from disability and onto God's abilit

Friday

Take Away

Generosity is mine to give and to receive.

Tuck Away

Give, and it will be given to you. A good measure, pressed down, s together and running over, will be poured into your lap. (Luke 6:

Give Away

I'll surprise a hurting mom with tokens of my concern—and pr grace when the roles are reversed.

notes

Each day of our lives we make depos
in the memory banks of our children.

Charles R. Swindoll

week 8

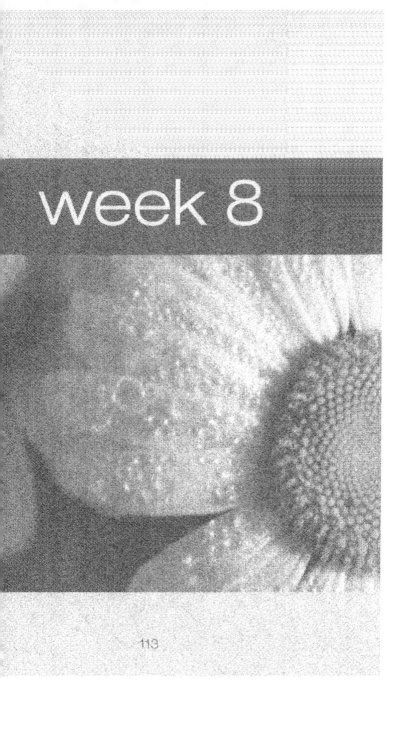

week 8

Testimony

Passing the Faith Along

I hope to visit you and talk with you face to face,
so that our joy may be complete.
2 John 12

"Grandma, are you happy at me?" granddaughter Becky occ ally asks. "I'm very happy with you," I assure her with a hug. I try by example to steer my grandchildren toward correct spe find myself charmed by their idiosyncratic expressions and irr grammatical constructions.

When I think about it, it's amazing what a difference an unass little preposition can make. Has it occurred to you, for instanc you can talk on three distinctly different levels? What differenc it make whether you talk *at*, *to*, or *with* someone else? Talk somebody is arguably the least effective form of communicati we can call it communication. It's what you do when you dress an ex-husband or teenage daughter about a forgotten promise infraction without pausing to hear their side of the story.

Talking *to* someone is a step up. The downside is that i a one-way affair where you rely on the other party's listening and assume he or she has nothing of value to contribute. Our an easily fall into this trap, especially since God's responses o be subtle, requiring time and effort to be "heard," let alone wledged and acted upon. And how often do you put forth the l and emotional energy to talk *with* someone, to engage in a ay sharing of ideas?

ive you faced the temptation to carry this "*with*" level of rsation too far with your kids (possibly the only available ng ears)? I made this mistake when Amanda was young, and rve Walter confiding at times with his little ones about fairly ty issues. These are exceptions, but generally you'll be surprised difference it makes when you make a point to communicate our kids. While you're at it, you might want to assure them rly that you're happy at them!

ach me, Lord, the beauty of reciprocal unication, both with you and with my children. us to develop a pattern of regular visiting face-to nd heart-to-heart, truly meeting with each other ry level. Amen.

ke Away: One-sided talks with my children and with God are not conversations.

week 8

Always Blessed

Traveling from Strength to Strengt

Blessed are those whose strength is in you, who ha
set their hearts on pilgrimage. They go from strengt
strength till each appears before God in Zion.
Psalm 84:5, 7

"How are you?" typically elicits one of a few stock answers. response that makes me smile comes regularly from the single who runs our office building's food service: "Always blessed."

The blessed person points her heart toward the lodestar o and follows it on a lifelong pilgrimage to his promised lan journey from oasis to oasis implies that she isn't there yet. B knows where she's going and is unafraid to walk through t times, knowing there's refreshment ahead.

I know that life for this young mother isn't always easy generally perky, but her response to the routine question "H you?" is never flip. Some days she replies with a rueful smil other mornings, genuinely appreciative of the interest, she to feeling tired or ruffled. I may be catching her between somewhere between strength and strength, somewhere on t side of rejuvenation. But she rightly assesses her situation by pc changeless condition in Christ.

e has learned to stand above her current position and glimpse
stretches of roadway ahead and behind. The literal meaning of
cond Hebrew clause of verse 5, in today's opening scripture
have set their hearts on pilgrimage"), is "on whose hearts are
highways"—toward Jerusalem for the celebration of religious
ls. My friend isn't detached from the nitty-gritty of daily life;
ttached to her source of strength. Because that Source is a Person
made promises to her, she's absolutely correct in pronouncing
f blessed.

ow happy you and I could be if we'd consistently view ourselves
d sees us, regardless of our circumstances. We're on Eternity
moving upward toward the New Jerusalem, traveling from rest
xation, sometimes stressed—but always blessed!

o be honest, Lord, I'm not always fine—but I don't o tell you that. Please remind me when I'm en route en strength and strength that your blessings flow errupted. Amen.

Take Away: No matter what my circumstances, I'm always blessed.

week 8

Becoming Less

Making Room for God

He must become greater; I must become less.
John 3:30

Isn't it amazing how each of us tends to view our universe, wh
its boundaries, with our self as its pivotal sun and center? We
like a bird, plume our feathers to appear more important; foc
enhancing our depleted self-image; or pamper ourselves, ass
(probably correctly) that no one else is going to do it for us.

Caring for and affirming yourself are necessary activities fo
physical and emotional well-being, but you as a Christian w
are wise not to take them too far. God created you with a need
noticed and appreciated. Beyond this, though, an insatiable
for status and recognition can be a danger sign.

I grew up in a home where humility was considered a ca
virtue, and for years my self-confidence level was low. A
today's younger generations the opposite is often true. The
who considers himself the center of attraction will go throu
expecting everyone and everything to submit to his gravita
pull. If separated or divorced parents, each flanked by an ext
family, compete for her affection, or if you're overcompensati

ss of her dad, you can create in your child a monster ego that :s constant feeding.

›d honors the meek (Matthew 5:5)—possibly as countercultural ıon in Jesus's day as it is in ours. If Christ is to expand in cance and influence in our lives, our grasping egos need to : to make room. If you truly allow the Spirit to grow within 'ou can be sure that others—including your kids—will take , both of you and of the Christ shining through you.

fear insignificance, Lord. But teach me that ing my ego will allow you more space to fill me yourself. Fill me up, Lord. Amen.

ake Away: I reserve for God that special place at the center of my self.

week 8

Dignity

Lips Anointed with Grace

"God . . . gives grace to the humble." Humble yourse
therefore, under God's mighty hand,
that he may lift you up in due time.
Cast all your anxiety on him because he cares for y
1 Peter 5:5–7

No matter how firmly you may stress to your kids that you anc estranged dad will likely not get back together, they may conti hold persistently to this fantasy. His remarriage not only intro a third parental and authority figure into an already-confusing tion but shatters a childish dream no other circumstance coul dislodged. If you've secretly harbored the same reunification the "happy" occasion sets in place a grieving process for bot and your kids.

It's one thing for you, suddenly the third party in an triangle, to welcome their stepmother with as much dignity can muster, but quite another to express permission for you to accept—even love?—this perceived rival. And giving emc consent for this "intruder" to take on a primary-caregiver rol t to your children, no matter what the custody arrangement, es a heaping helping of grace. Like it or not, though, God s us to respond in precisely this manner.

alm 45 (ironically, a wedding song) refers in verse 2 to lips that been anointed with grace." The reference is to the groom/king. ike has similar words about Jesus: "All . . . were amazed at the us words that came from his lips" (Luke 4:22). Each of us as a ian woman has received an anointing; we've been empowered gh Christ's Spirit with gracious lips and hearts that can see us gh even the most trying situations we'll encounter.

may help to remember that you're never the "odd woman vith God. Your confusion, pain, and anxiety are at any given nt his number one priority, and he waits for you to seek the he longs to lavish on you.

noint my lips and heart, Lord, with the power of grace. Accept my load of anxiety, for with it my love and trust. Amen.

ke Away: With God's help I can approach difficult situations with grace.

week 8

Avoidance

Finding the Help You Need

My friends and companions avoid me because of r
wounds; my neighbors stay far away.
Come quickly to help me, O Lord my Savior.
Psalm 38:11, 22

Our self-absorbed culture shouts the message that no one l complainer. Many single moms with significant needs and coı are afraid of coming off as whiners. You may downplay or your needs, seeing those of others as more legitimate and impo Afraid of having others avoid you, you may avoid intimacy.

My kids' circumstances have often been unique to a po sounding bizarre. When friends, church members, and cow ask how things are going, I feel uncomfortable if I relate too detail. Yet I sometimes find it difficult to stop myself, and into the limelight before I can curtail my impulsivity. At other (when I'm loneliest and neediest), I'm tempted to function as a cutting off all but the most necessary communication.

I've found individual therapy helpful since it provid appropriate outlet for "telling all." Pastoral counseling is a alternative. In addition, you could probably find one or two t

ı members who would be happy to lend a listening ear and a
g hand. If this hasn't been your experience, or if you've been
rately steering clear of relationships with other Christians, you
want to force yourself to actively seek this fellowship.

ur friends and acquaintances really may be avoiding you (if
ehavior is standoffish or overly negative or emotional, making
uncomfortable), but it's well possible that your perception is
d.

otice that the psalmist wasn't hesitant to call upon the Lord
ne quickly to his aid. And God's Word guarantees that he'll
ıd when you make the same request. Through the Bible he
you his personal comfort, and he can open your eyes to areas in
your own shame, misperception, or misguided approach may
sing you difficulty.

n not sure whether others avoid me or whether I put off. Lord, help me to discard whatever stands en me and the love you long to give to me through Amen.

ke Away: I resolve to be open with others
en they express an interest in my situation.

week 8

Wrap It Up

Monday

Take Away

One-sided talks with my children and with God are not convers

Tuck Away

Let your conversation be always full of grace, seasoned with (Colossians 4:6)

Give Away

When dialoguing with my friend, I'll season my words with a sprinkling of grace.

Tuesday

Take Away

No matter what my circumstances, I'm always blessed.

Tuck Away

Praise the LORD, *O my soul, and forget not all his benefits. He . . . me with love and compassion. He satisfies my desires with good* (Psalm 103:2–5)

Away

ss along God's blessings to me; sharing won't diminish their lance.

dnesday

Away

ve for God that special place at the center of my self.

Away

thing out of selfish ambition or vain conceit, but in humility con- thers better than yourselves. Each of you should look not only to your terests, but also to the interests of others. (Philippians 2:3–4)

Away

athe a prayer when speaking with that depleted single mom: r up, Lord!"

rsday

Away

God's help I can approach difficult situations with grace.

Away

uard over my mouth, O Lord; keep watch over the door of my lips. my heart be drawn to what is evil. (Psalm 141:3–4)

Give Away

Anointed with God's grace, I'll speak and act reflectivel
receptively.

Friday

Take Away

I resolve to be open with others when they express an interest
situation.

Tuck Away

Wounds from a friend can be trusted. Do not forsake your
(Proverbs 27:6, 10)

Give Away

When it comes to the hurts and complications in others' liv
curtail my own tendency to avoid others in need.

notes

There are two lasting bequests we can g
our children. One is roots.
The other is wings.

Hodding Carter Jr.

week 9

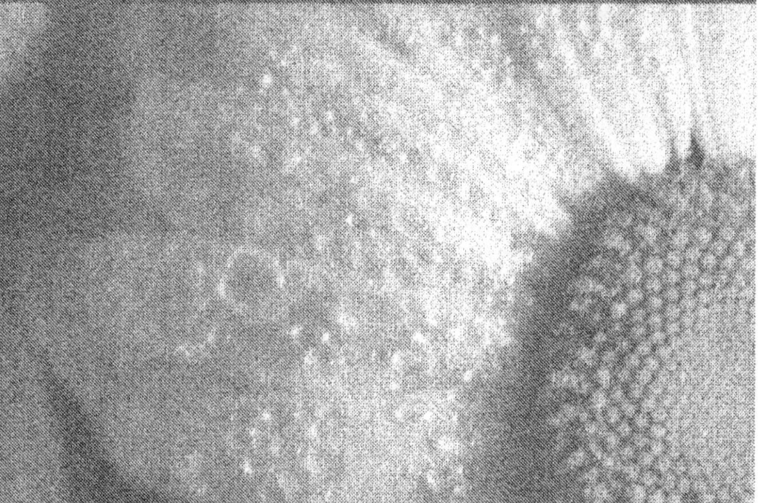

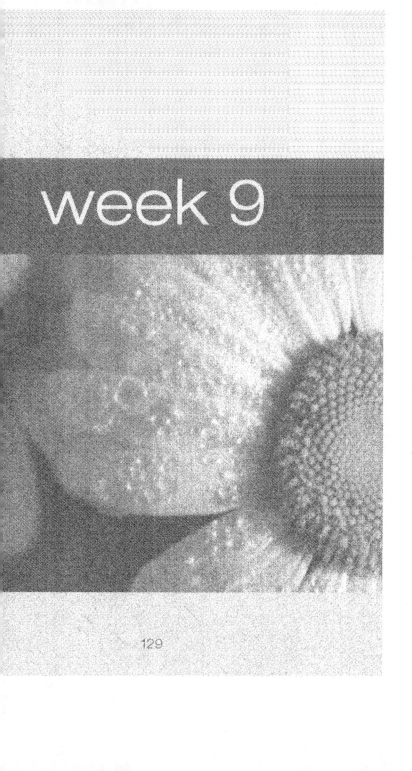

week 9

Burdens

Resting on His Shoulders

The one the LORD loves rests between his shoulde

Deuteronomy 33:12

Ever notice that a chip on your shoulder is heavier than you have suspected? Whether your anger is directed at someone hurt you (maybe an ex-husband), society, or the system, ch are, you're the only one being hurt by that chafing, back-bre grudge.

If a chip is heavy, a yoke must weigh a ton. Yet Jesus invite to try his on for size, referring to it as "easy" and "light" (Ma 11:28–30) and associating it with soul rest. Has it ever occur you that a yoke is meant for two? Jesus's yoke is light only if your side, pulling for you and teaching you the ropes of the Chr life.

Speaking of rest—and shoulders—have you ever happened the verse above? I picture a shepherd with a lamb slung ov shoulders, firmly but gently grasping its legs. During those when you're not fit for active training, when even Jesus's ligh easy yoke is too heavy for your overstrained shoulders, you can him to give you a lift. You'll get optimal benefit from the r willing to let go of that chip first. Your unfinished business can f your back if you make the effort, with God's help, to confront ssues and leave them behind.

ul asks us in Galatians 6:2 to carry each other's burdens. ces are, your baggage won't feel heavy to me, especially with the edge that you're helping to shoulder my load. A shared burden nes much more than 50 percent lighter for either party. Don't e it? Give it a try.

e wondered, Lord, at the total release of a baby in my arms. Mold me into your embrace, I until I can let myself go with the same degree of ion. Amen.

Take Away: Jesus relieves me of my load of care.

week 9

Higher Thoughts

Soaring in the Stratosphere

As the heavens are higher than the earth,
so are my ways higher than your ways
and my thoughts than your thoughts.
Isaiah 55:9

Ever wish you could reallocate some resources and rearrange situations? Ever feel as though Murphy's Law has displaced th of averages—and that God's law, his rule over all things, is cc in a distant third?

I don't actually believe that, but Isaiah points out in the verse that even my fleeting doubts on the subject may indicate a pro God's will for us is perfect, although he doesn't force us to foll When we don't, though, we suffer natural consequences. Stil doesn't stop God from working in and through our circums to bring out the good (Romans 8:28). "I know the plans I ha you," he gently reminds us, "plans to prosper you and not to you, plans to give you hope and a future" (Jeremiah 29:11).

During certain passages of your life, possibly after divo death has spun your world out of control, words like *prosper*, and *future* may bring out more cynicism in you than encourage ay respond like Sarah, laughing in a scornful senior moment at ospect of giving birth (Genesis 18:10–12).

rew up in Southern California, and although I left years ago, ember the inversion layer, caused by atmospheric pressure, ng down the smog, choking my valley. I still live in a sinful world, omething like that inversion layer is grounding my thoughts. od's thoughts are soaring free in the stratosphere, rolling and ng in delight on my—and your—behalf. I'd like to say "the he limit" in his designs for me. But the reality is infinitely more tic—"out of this world," to put it mildly. Maybe I'll just rest ad for a while and leave the thinking to him!

ank you, Lord, for the span of your thoughts and ach of your love toward me. Remind me that no ge of life can carry me beyond the reception of your and care. Amen.

Take Away: My Father knows best.

week 9

Pricey Love

Engraved on God's Hands

Can a mother forget the baby at her breast and hav
compassion on the child she has borne? Though s
may forget, I will not forget you! See, I have engrav
you on the palms of my hands.
Isaiah 49:15–16

Isaiah's question in the first sentence, above, sounds rhetorical obvious and even outraged answer being *No!* But the prophet's ing statement reflects that he wasn't so naive as to fail to rec that every rule has its exceptions. Unfortunately, in our society, are many.

I've seen this unthinkable kind of abandonment happen three daughters. And I've seen one of them, when she was and married, make the same choice. Depressed, mentally il overwhelmed by the demands of three babies, she simply w away, first repeatedly and then finally.

Maybe you've witnessed similar behavior in your kids' dad simply exited your family situation, without so much as a bac glance, how did you explain his motives to them? Or possib yourself have wrestled with whether or not it was in your best i k or maintain custody. Maybe you've found it convenient to ch a difficult or troubled kid to his or her other parent to w well *he or she* could do. Such circumstances are invariably lex, and the blame game usually ends in a draw. But Isaiah t the very least, right in suggesting that a mom *may* forget her

s point, though, is that God will not—indeed, based on the ity of his nature, *cannot*—forget you. The closest analogy I can of to engraving someone's name on the palm of your hand is o—it's a good idea to be sure of a relationship before taking ep. But God hasn't engraved your *name* on the palms of his ; he's permanently etched your *self* there. That makes you ingly—indelibly—unforgettable to him!

ngraving me on your hands cost you something er, just as the nails in his palms cost your Son. pricey love is eternal. Help me to make it forever it. Amen.

Take Away: God will never abandon or forget me.

week 9

Inside-Out

Reflecting His Beauty

[Your beauty] should be that of your inner self, th
unfading beauty of a gentle and quiet spirit, which is
great worth in God's sight.
1 Peter 3:4

Do you ever find that, while you're attracted to particularly b ful people, you tend to distrust and perhaps even dislike then intrigued when I read Isaiah's past-tense description of the yet- born Jesus: "He had no beauty or majesty to attract us to him. . . one from whom men hide their faces he was despised" (Isaiah 53 Ouch! Was Jesus deformed in some way or simply ordinary?

Let's face it, many of us are repulsed by the idea of our average. You may yearn to stand out—generally in terms of physical appearance—in some positive way. For you as a single this craving might be increased by low self-esteem, if you feel been dumped.

The apostle Peter spoke about a beauty that doesn't r preservation, an appeal so much a part of who you are t becomes a permanent distinctive that others immediately ass with you. Identify some women you know who reflect "a gent

spirit." Are you attracted to them? Do you seek them out on
per, possibly even spiritual, level? Now take an inventory of
appearance. Chances are, they vary widely in terms of age, size,
shape, and other physical characteristics. How much has this
red to you in pursuing their counsel and companionship?

rtainly, it's good to keep yourself up, to look and feel your
able best. But your core appeal has to do with your essence,
enter. Real beauty is an inside-out proposition; that's the way
designed you. The physical Jesus may have lacked outward
iveness, but the Christ inside you wants to shine through you
ll the splendor of eternity. You're at your most beautiful when
low yourself to reflect his loveliness.

*ur value system, Christ, seems topsy-turvy to
nside out and upside down. Yet recalling it keeps
rspective right side up. Help me to focus on your
y rather than my own—and allow it to shine forth
gh me. Amen.*

ke Away: My beauty secret is Jesus in me.

week 9

Agreeable Disagreement

A Healthful Nighttime Ritual

"In your anger do not sin": Do not let the sun go do
while you are still angry,
and do not give the devil a foothold.
Ephesians 4:26–27

My parents have lived their married life by the credo of Eph 4:26, making sure to resolve any lingering disagreements nigh fore retiring. Not that they always agree, but they agree to dis agreeably. Whether you've been lambasted by an ex-spouse, sn by a coworker, or criticized by a sibling, chances are, your most ductive" seething time comes after lights out. How restorative i sleep on those nights?

The apostle Paul in the verse above was quoting Psalm 4: your anger do not sin; when you are on your beds, search your and be silent." Anger is an emotion, not a sin—a God-given valve for pent-up tensions in danger of detonating. But, if h incorrectly, if nursed and cultivated for your private satisfactio potentially vindictive emotion leaves your heart vulnerable to s its most militant promoter.

How often have you lain in bed rehearsing the brilliant con

vish you had made, carefully strategizing a counterattack, ɛefully awaiting daylight to pounce on your unsuspecting ɪent? The psalmist's injunction to "search your hearts" is a ɛnt proposition altogether. Heart (or soul) searching might in unwanted complications—like misgivings, guilt, empathy, esire to forgive or make peace.

e next time your teenager screams at you at bedtime, try an ment. Allow her to vent, then lock your door if you can. pt to tune out her stomping feet and blaring music, and invite irit to help you understand. You may still plan a response (not a on) to carry out in the morning. Later, when she's approachable, t a mutual strategy of refusing to go to sleep angry. You might prised at the outcome.

ank you, Lord, for each of my emotions; they're ctive parts of your image in me. But safeguard me against allowing any of them to take control over sential me. Amen.

ake Away: I can resolve volatile situations before the day ends.

week 9

Wrap It Up

Monday

Take Away

Jesus relieves me of my load of care.

Tuck Away

My guilt has overwhelmed me like a burden too heavy to O Lord, do not forsake me; be not far from me, O my God. (
38:4, 21)

Give Away

Unencumbered myself, I'll help to shoulder my fr
burden.

Tuesday

Take Away

My Father knows best.

Tuck Away

Many, O Lord my God, are the wonders you have done. The thir planned for us no one can recount to you; were I to speak and them, they would be too many to declare. (Psalm 40:5)

saturday

Away

ɔare with my distracted, distraught friend that God's hts toward her are his top priority.

dnesday

Away

vill never abandon or forget me.

Away

made you, . . . I will not forget you. . . . Return to me, for I have ed you. (Isaiah 44:21–22)

Away

ure my neighbor that God holds her close—not just her name, e, or memory but her very self.

rsday

Away

auty secret is Jesus in me.

Away

ver is true, whatever is noble, whatever is right, whatever is pure, ver is lovely, whatever is admirable—if anything is excellent or vorthy—think about such things. (Philippians 4:8)

Give Away

With God's help I'll think and do what's beautiful to Him.

Friday

Take Away

I can resolve volatile situations before the day ends.

Tuck Away

You were once darkness, but now you are light in the Lord. Live a
dren of light. Find out what pleases the Lord. (Ephesians 5:8, 10

Give Away

When my friend and I are at odds, I'll seek resolution with a
(as in today!) visit, call, or e-mail.

notes

*No matter how calmly
you try to referee, parenting will
eventually produce bizarre behavior, a
I'm not talking about the kids.*

Bill Cosby

week 10

week 10

Identity

The Root of the Matter

If the root is holy, so are the branches.
Romans 11:16

College freshmen in my Philosophy 101 class struggled with ceptively difficult assignment: to define a *thing*. I still avoid the in my writing. A similarly slippery term is *matter*. "What's the ter?" you probe, meaning, "What's the problem?" "It doesn't m you insist, implying, "It's not important." "This better be a of life or death," you fume when your child bangs on the bath door as soon as you step into the shower.

The expression "the root of the madder" (which evolve time into our familiar "the root of the matter") has a pr history. In the pioneering days of the American West, homeste craving color in their drab lives, included in their gardens a called *madder*. Its value was in its root, which produced a burnt orange dye.

Your life may seem like a hopelessly tangled, untended But underneath you're more than someone "with a past." Y unique individual with a long, continuous history full of sw and swathes of rich color and vibrancy.

hat words define you? If adjectives like *single, gullible, messed burned out*, or nouns like *divorcée, used goods,* or *idiot* flash your screen, flip the channel. Such words or phrases describe rceptions or realities about your *situation*—not *you.* They're the own branches begging to be trimmed.

a recent self-enrichment exercise at work, each participant was ted with a sheet of factual or positive adjectives. We were asked ct five that best described us. It was surprisingly difficult to v down the choices. Who you are, at the root, has to do with underlying character qualities that make you special. Why not blank sheet with positive words that describe you—the same at God created in his image.

laster Gardener, I invite you to tend and trim back ne. But above all, please supply my roots with your and steady supply of living water. Amen.

Take Away: I won't confuse my identity with my situation.

week 10

Dusty Cobwebs

Redeemed and Transformed

[God] has made everything beautiful in its time.
Ecclesiastes 3:11

My sons-in-law were refinishing my kitchen cupboard doors basement. The sanding process had generated quite a layer of and they had asked me not to stir this up until the last coat of urethane had dried—a rationale for procrastination with which happy to comply.

At one point I stepped into their workroom to check pr The doors were beautiful, but I was more intrigued by the c Hanging from the exposed rafters was a labyrinth of cobwebs delicate thread outlined and highlighted by a layer of fine dus unexpected sight was momentarily breathtaking.

Cobwebs and dust. The stuff of beauty? At least temp yes. If our original foreparents hadn't succumbed to temptati wouldn't be sweeping webs from basement rafters. But God do things that allow beauty to triumph against all odds: he redeer he transforms.

God buys back or takes back aspects of creation to allow to prevail in a sin-damaged world. You may have felt dirty ıath of a messy divorce, but he chose you and pulled you back the grunge. Why? For *him* and for his glory. And because he you. After God reclaims, he also transforms. He changes the of something (like dust or your heart).

ɔd wasn't responsible for your drifting off in the first place. he wants you back, you can't stop him from redeeming and orming you. You can help, though, by moving toward him. No what your past, he wants you. He made you from dust, and needs to, he'll use cobwebs and dust to make you startlingly ful for his pleasure and for your benefit. Trust him!

hank you, my Redeemer, for sifting through the of a fallen creation to find me, take me back to elf, and shine me up, inside and out. May we find ıl pleasure as we love and appreciate one another. n.

Take Away: God claims me and cleans me up for his pleasure.

week 10

Provider

One-Symptom Appointment?

Those who seek the LORD lack no good thing.
Psalm 34:10

I recently made a quickie appointment with my doctor's PA (p
cian's assistant). To streamline the process I jotted down my co
and handed the paper to the nurse. Her matter-of-fact respons
sorry. This is a one-symptom appointment."

Have you noticed that you no longer have a doctor, bab
or insurance agent? Instead, you deal with a list of "prov
some of whom may appear to be too preoccupied for much q
providing.

God, of course, is our consummate, capital *P* Provider. But
PA is too busy within my allotted time slot to process more th
"complaint," it's easy for me to assume that God must be too.
the world's exploding population and the increased rate of b
marriages and other stressors that may impact *your* situation
too, may feel compelled to keep your appointments with God
and to the point.

Isn't it refreshing when a doctor enjoys chatting? Mu
the conversation may be professionally driven: she may w

nventory of circumstances conceivably affecting your blood re. But it's gratifying when you sense her kicking back, cally, mentally, and emotionally, to spend a few moments just cting.

od has all the time in the world (in fact, time only *affects* this). He wants nothing more than a drawn-out daily chat with ven if you're washing dishes while you talk. Feel free to discuss ver concerns or joys, large or small, are on your mind. Pauses you daydream or address a child are fine too. They give him a e to respond. God makes no one-symptom appointments—no itments, period. He's on call just for you, 24/7.

"time" isn't an operative word for you, Lord, you have a schedule too hectic to fit me in. Thank you I don't need to worry about bothering you with my petty concerns—four more earthbound words that nothing in the vocabulary of heaven. Amen.

ake Away: God's never too busy for me.

week 10

Overcommitment

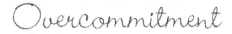

Summarizing the Outline

Let the beloved of the LORD rest secure in him,
for he shields [her] all day long.
Deuteronomy 33:12

In high school Khris checked out library books on obscure su
but downplayed homework, grades, and assignments. In a rare
of discipline during her senior year, she worked at home on a
paper. I was pleased to catch a fleeting glimpse of a lengthy ou
Unfortunately, her spurt of resolution had dwindled to an oc
the ninth hour of writing the paper. But Khris was "finished"
cord time. She flashed before me two pages of double-spaced
"*No worries*, Mom!" She rolled her eyes. "I summarized the ou
No, she didn't misspeak. Khris didn't expand the outline: it w
nificantly longer than her paper.

Do you find yourself wanting to make up to your kids fo
dad's absence? To fill both parental roles? To fill your calendar (ou
based on high ideals—and hopeless overcommitment? You ma
the discipline, stamina, organization, or ability to estimate the
resource ratio needed to follow through with your plan. Yo

: in various ventures, quickly losing interest or momentum. ay burn yourself out . . . or summarize (pick and choose from) utline (to-do list).

an incurable list keeper, but I've learned to keep my outline t, fleshing it out with reachable objectives. On a recent Saturday enda was fluid enough to allow time for a needed three-hour still managed to accomplish what was necessary, and I spent f the evening knitting a scarf in front of the TV.

ou're the driven type, you can learn to say no to overbooking lf. Maybe you can even surprise your kids with a clean-slate, fternoon. You'll be happier, healthier, and more relaxed for it.

e confused my work ethic with my faith, Lord.
alendar's daily outline of excellent intentions was
ength just by my looking at it. Help me to define
eet realistic goals, leaving enough blanks for
g family time and personal down time. Amen.

Take Away: My tendency to overcommit helps no one.

week 10

Memories

Blessing Your Family

Then all the people left, each for his own home, and David returned home to bless his family.
1 Chronicles 16:43

I'm intrigued by the turn of phrase in the final clause of this Scr nugget. It's startling and a little elusive. When I head home end of a long day, I typically have an agenda. As often as not I' hurry to work my way through the "have to's" to reach my ult goal—precious time to kick back and relax in one way or anot

If you're like me, you think of *blessing* as a God thing, a on benefit emanating from him toward you and those you love. blessings—from the gift of breath to the relief of breathing sp are absolutely critical to your survival and happiness. Contr our usual model, though, blessing is a two-way street.

When I was quite young, my dad worked twenty-four-hou at the fire department, leaving my mom "single" a fair amo the time. One Sunday afternoon after dinner, Debbie and delighted to learn that Mom had planned a surprise. She'd pieces of cardboard and devoted the afternoon to making dol furniture with us. Mom died when I was eleven, and my memo e limited. But I do recall that afternoon she blessed me!

ow can you deliberately bless your kids? This might be as simple iping out on your living-room floor on a Friday night. Or as s as an in-depth discussion of the reasons for your faith. This of activity requires an extra-energy expenditure. It's proactive, innovative, above and beyond the routine. But you might be sed at how far above and beyond life's norm your loving act ake your kids. Chances are, they'll remember your blessing all ives.

od of all blessing, help me as your personal entative to deliberately bless those closest to me—my Amen.

e Away: With a little creative planning, I can ess my kids with a memorable experience.

week 10

Wrap It Up

Monday

Take Away

I won't confuse my identity with my situation.

Tuck Away

Search me, O God, and know my heart; test me and know my a
thoughts. See if there is any offensive way in me, and lead me in t
everlasting. (Psalm 139:23–24)

Give Away

I'll help my friend to separate her circumstances from the esse
herself.

Tuesday

Take Away

God claims me and cleans me up for his pleasure.

Tuck Away

The Spirit of the Sovereign L*ORD* *is on me. . . . He has sent me t*
up the brokenhearted, . . . to bestow on them a crown of beauty
of ashes. (Isaiah 61:1–3)

Away

my friend feels dirty, degraded, or despondent, I'll share the
of how God claimed, cleansed, and cherishes me.

dnesday

Away

never too busy for me.

Away

*ful always; pray continually; give thanks in all circumstances, for
God's will for you in Christ Jesus.* (1 Thessalonians 5:16–18)

Away

re with another single mom the news of God's open and direct
contact—while expressing my own concern for her.

rsday

Away

ndency to overcommit helps no one.

Away

with me by yourselves to a quiet place and get some rest. (Mark

Give Away

I'll carve out priority time for befriending and encouraging n
pleted neighbor.

Friday

Take Away

With a little creative planning, I can bless my kids with a mem
experience.

Tuck Away

If you then, though you are evil, know how to give good gifts to you dren, how much more will your Father in heaven give the Holy Sp those who ask him! (Luke 11:13)

Give Away

My family and I will include another single-parent family i
great adventures.

notes

Instant availability without continuou
presence is probably the
best role a mother can play.

Lotte Bailyn

week 11

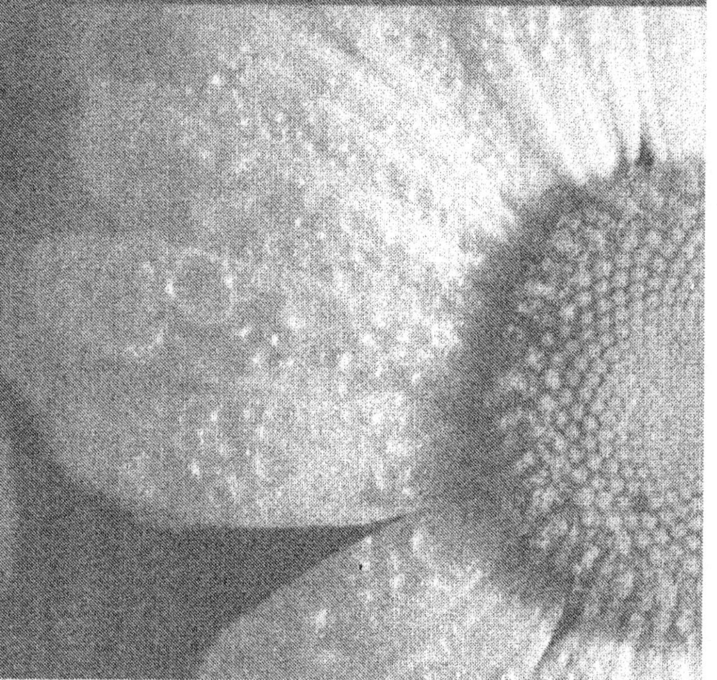

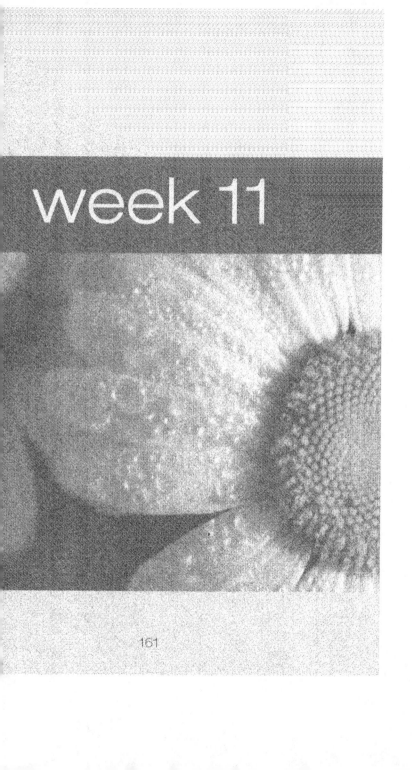

week 11

Singleness

Gnawing on the Styrofoam?

To the unmarried and the widows I say:
It is good for them to stay unmarried, as I am.
1 Corinthians 7:8

Some time ago I handed my then one-year-old grandson T Styrofoam cup filled with cheesy goldfish. Almost immed he proceeded to pour out the crackers and nibble contentec the cup. I *do* know how to give good gifts to my grandchildr Matthew 7:10 Jesus even uses *fish* as an example). But I can't them to recognize them as such. What about you? How is you record for identifying and utilizing God's good gifts?

Take your singleness. An extreme example? Maybe. Paul think so (bear in mind that his observations were in no way int to carry authority): "An unmarried woman . . . is concerned the Lord's affairs: Her aim is to be devoted to the Lord in botl and spirit" (1 Corinthians 7:34).

Your energy level and zeal for the Lord may not match Paul he wasn't encumbered (er, blessed) with your kids. But God call *you* to be the "apostle to the Gentiles." He may have called . . . bless your family. This seems to be true for me. My adult cl resent seemingly endless challenges. But I take comfort from nviction that they (along with my son-in-law and ex-son-in- onstitute a significant part of my mission opportunity. The children are a wonderful bonus who will no doubt also present nges as they grow.

e single life may be exactly the last state you'd have opted for. If el this way, by all means continue to pray for a mate. But why ke some time while you're at it to evaluate your role in the lives r children and others. Is it just possible that you've poured out good "fish" to gnaw on Styrofoam?

e been lifting up my prayer for a godly mate for time now, Lord. I want to accede to your will but ng for this connection. In the meantime, please help accurately assess my current situation and identify hand of blessing. Amen.

Take Away: God may be calling me to remain single.

week 11

Following Through

Taking the Plunge

May [the LORD] give you the desire of your heart
and make all your plans succeed.
Psalm 20:4

Five frogs sat on a lily pad. Three decided to jump off. How were left? FIVE. Just because they decided to jump doesn't they did.

Actually, the need to make a decision can represent a di hurdle in and of itself. The follow-through may, in some cases relatively simple in comparison. At other times, resolution fo up by exactly nothing may leave us feeling frustrated and v guilty.

What short- or long-range decisions have you made re Have you thought of recommitting yourself to church atte and involvement? Purchasing a home? Taking night courses to bachelor's or master's degree? Seeking a license as a day-care pr Becoming more involved with your child's school? Being positive in talking with your kids about their dad?

Unproductive habits, when broken, can move you an family in the direction of mending battered hearts and lives nd that decisions don't always require—or necessarily allow immediate execution. But there's almost always a place to start. liminary juggling of circumstances might leave you poised to rom your overcrowded launching pad.

critical first step is determining whether a decision or resolution rs to be in line with God's will. Countless books have been n on this subject. But the bottom line is, if you're alert and God will often clear (or obstruct) your path.

eams, goals, hard work, and prayer—all critical components oving forward in life. Even if you're inching forward, you're d in the right direction. And the inspiration itself will positively your outlook and motivation. So ready? Set? LEAP! And have a idventure while you're at it.

e made some critical decisions, Lord—already l step for me. Now grant me the grace and ge to follow through in increments. Remind me to ually test your will as I move—or even shuffle rd. Amen.

ke Away: God guides me in setting goals and working on resolutions.

week 11

Lifeline

God's Resourceful Spirit

Teach me to do your will, for you are my God;
may your good Spirit lead me on level ground.
For your name's sake, O Lord, preserve my life;
in your righteousness, bring me out of trouble.
Psalm 143:10–11

Dinner was in progress, and Walt, the children, and I were ben our plates. "Look!" Walter Jr. squealed without preamble. Four rose in unison, and five pairs of eyes locked, transfixed, on a spe unfolding inches from our faces. A single strand from an unsee had dropped from a blade of the ceiling fan, and its occupan clinging tenaciously to this lifeline, was being whipped arour table. Too surprised at this absurd exhibition to turn off the f adults broke the frozen silence by unison laughter. The thre dlers, opting in kind for humor as opposed to fear, began to c with us in delight.

At that moment an equally unforeseen development sobere the little ones: the spider, evidently sensing an adverse circums began methodically to inch its way back up the silken strand—

p to the blade from which it had plummeted.

either you nor I are privy to the thought patterns of the smaller of creatures, if, indeed, whatever synapses occur in those pinprick qualify as thoughts. But of one fact I felt convicted: that spider unk. In addition, her single strand of a web, apparently in the tages of construction, withheld remarkably well against the ugal force working against it.

hen have you felt yourself, as a solo mom, hanging on—to ial solvency, family cohesiveness, or even to life or "sanity"—as by a thread? Looking back, did you, like that unpretentious, rown spider above my table, grope or scrabble your way back a level plane under your own power or through your own cefulness? Or, as David pleaded so eloquently in Psalm 143, ur Creator/Father's "good Spirit" lead you on, or to, level l?

ood Spirit, I ask you to keep me and my family moving forward on a horizontal plane. At the time, keep us in close touch with the vertical, able to l with your help above life's troubles. Amen.

e Away: I can rely on the preserving power of God's resourceful Spirit.

week 11

Holiday Loneliness

God's Horizontal Approach

Turn to me and be gracious to me, for I am lonely

Psalm 25:16

A coworker shared with me a poignant story about her hus He'd been alone, and lonely, for fifteen years prior to their ma the second for both. On more than one Christmas, he had pur and tucked away a gift-wrapped woman's item—only to ret after the holiday.

I was less selfless. For a number of years, while my girl growing up, I would "find" under our tree a beautifully wr sweater or blouse, tagged to myself from a Secret Admire daughters, I learned only recently, had been duly impressed.

Loneliness, or simply a deprivation of caring, can hit u when the holidays roll around. The allure of Christmas so brings out the child in us. Hand in hand with the spiritual wo this blessed time, the human side is supposed to fulfill us too, The angel's words reverberate in our aching souls: "On earth p [those] on whom his favor rests."

If you're like me, you want that peace. You want it in a ta personal, *now* kind of way. And that's OK! God often approa ntally, sidling up to us quietly. He comes through people we uch, particularly at this vulnerable time of year.

sides your kids, who has God provided to share his blessed his year with you? If you're drawing a blank, has it occurred to take the initiative with another single person? You may have le for companionship in lieu of romance. But chances are that ne, male or female, would love to share some mutual joy with he connection might even enhance your new year.

nd, crowds and reunions over the holiday season my aloneness excruciating by contrast. Help me, y, to seek and find, as part of your Christmas y, a kindred spirit. Then envelop us in peace as we er, celebrate your Son. Amen.

Take Away: One plus one equals zero lonely people.

week 11

Significance

The Gifts of Time and Memory

Remember your Creator in the days of your yout
Ecclesiastes 12:1

When my mom was growing up in Depression-era Grand R Michigan, her dad worked in a department store. Unable t chase Christmas gifts for his five children, he opted for o temporary joy. With permission from store management, he lavishly surround the family Christmas tree with presents—o until December 26. This gesture seemed to me, when I heard it, more heartless than heartwarming. But these children no understood that their blessing came in the form of *time*—a revel in opulent bliss—and irreplaceable *memories*.

God wants you to be happy. But how easy is it for you into the trap of equating that elusive emotion with the givi acquisition of material goods? This may be particularly true view your kids as deprived because of your single-parent status a need to vie with, or outdo, their dad and his extended famil

I doubt that your family's blessing one another on the Christ's birth displeases God. But might he be more deligh gifts of time spent with your family and meaningful holiday ons that will result in indelible memories? One caveat: you're o make certain that the blessings you offer are truly about those l people in your life and not about your own ego.

your kids understand that their "big gift" is God's Son? Do you or special, unique ways to foster and enhance a sense of wonder ist's coming? If you can lead your children to "remember" their r/Savior already in the days of their childhood and youth, how greater the probability that this early pattern will stand them in tead throughout all of the Christmases—and the everydays— r lives!

ather of the Christ child, help me this Christmas n my family in the direction of a meaningful and able celebration of his birth. Keep the blessings of nd memory foremost in my mind as I formulate g plans for my own children. Amen.

ake Away: Focusing on quality time and meaningful traditions makes my Christmas more memorable.

week 11

Wrap It Up

Monday

Take Away

God may be calling me to remain single.

Tuck Away

I urge you to live a life worthy of the calling you have received. T
one body and one Spirit. But to each one of us grace has been g
Christ apportioned it. (Ephesians 4:1, 4, 7)

Give Away

I'll shore up my friend's confidence in her *self*, whether or no
backed up by, or backing up, a mate or significant other.

Tuesday

Take Away

God guides me in setting goals and working on resolutions.

Tuck Away

[She] who trusts in the L*ORD* *will prosper.* (Proverbs 28:25)

Away

my friend finds herself entrenched or immobilized, I'll help
out and commit to a plan of action.

dnesday

Away

ely on the preserving power of God's resourceful Spirit.

Away

*hteous cry out, and the LORD hears them; he delivers them from
r troubles. The LORD is close to the brokenhearted and saves those
e crushed in spirit.* (Psalm 34:17–18)

Away

my acquaintance is barely hanging on, I will, with the Spirit's
lp her to begin her ascent.

rsday

Away

lus one equals zero lonely people.

Away

e better than one. . . . If one falls down, [her] friend can help [her]
clesiastes 4:9–10)

Give Away

I'll invite someone else to share my holiday who might oth
find herself dining alone.

Friday

Take Away

Focusing on quality time and meaningful traditions mak
Christmas more memorable.

Tuck Away

Even when I am old and gray, do not forsake me, O God, till I
your power to the next generation, your might to all who are to
(Psalm 71:18)

Give Away

By sharing my faith and traditions, I'll help a floundering
embrace Christ's birthday in a new and meaningful way.

notes

To us, family means putting your arm
around each other and being there.

Barbara Bush

week 12

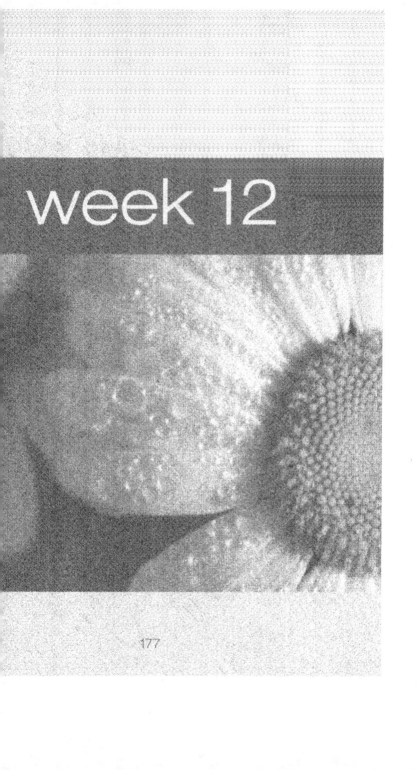

week 12

God's Shield

He Stoops to Make You Great

Who is like the LORD our God,
the One who sits enthroned on high,
who stoops down to look on the heavens and the ea
Psalm 113:5–6

A mother bending over to examine the ladybug in her child turned palm. Jesus stooping to wash Peter's feet (John 13:4– to write with his finger on the ground (John 8:8). The verb connotes gentleness, humility, meekness. A stooping posture opposite of a threatening or arrogant pose.

When God stoops to look on our Earth, he's not compensati nearsightedness. In fact, if he had a body, he could quite legiti rock back and forth on his heels, arms akimbo, glowering injustices taking place on our miserable little planet.

God *is* intensely interested in the details of your life, th Picture him crouching attentively, elbow propped on knee well-loved "thinker" pose, thoroughly engrossed in the daily of activities of an unassuming single mom and her kids. May other hand is extended, not to manipulate you, but to brush pollution or protect you from danger.

llowing deliverance from Saul, the psalmist David sang a song ise to God. Listen in: "You give me your shield of victory; you down to make me great. You broaden the path beneath me, so ny ankles do not turn" (2 Samuel 22:36–37).

ext time you feel insignificant, isolated, or forgotten, imagine bending over you, gently brushing away debris from your path vent a mishap that might hamper your ability to function. Your isn't been without its problems (any more than David's was), ou're great in the sight of your Creator/Father. He's willing to ou *his own* shield—or whatever else it takes—to ensure your eing.

reator/Father, sometimes I feel like an ant, ing about my hillock over a sidewalk crack. Yet w that you delight in and admire even the least of creatures. Thanks for constantly hovering over me h solicitous care. Amen.

Take Away: I bask in my Protector's undivided attention.

week 12

Never Alone

Solutions for Solitude?

I will never leave you nor forsake you.
Joshua 1:5

A survey asked eight- and nine-year-olds to propose solutions f world's pervasive loneliness problem. One out-of-the-box th proposed access to talking food as a solution. Another suggeste everyone be provided with a pet—or a husband! A girl sug an Internet match-up between self-proclaimed lonely and non people. A boy, admitting to sometimes feeling unloved, sug doing what he does to counteract this unpleasant perception stomp his feet—or read.

These ideas are worth a chuckle—or a tear. The truth is, th that you may have tried them. Chances are, you don't di silence, even when alone. Who of us isn't accustomed, after endless, surround-sound noise? Pets stave off isolation. Qu marriages keep some previously unattached individuals conn for good or ill. And Internet dating services and chat rooms companionship superstore accessible at the touch of a finger the comfort of home. You're reading right now (one of my pe

:e activities). And you might at times stomp your feet and go ic—a concession allowed lonesome, frustrated people.

r years my social circle revolved around other single moms with ters around the ages of my own. In nearly every case, though, girls grew up, they (and eventually, we moms as well) grew Today I enjoy acquaintances at work and church but have only ous few real friends.

I lonely? Sometimes. Fortunately, I'm something of a ody who enjoys thoughtful silence. How about you? There's e-all for this dilemma, nor does God promise to remove the m. But he does provide a coping mechanism, a fail-safe source solation: God cares!

love my kids, Lord, but at times I crave social notional stimulation beyond their ability to give. I know your long-term designs for my life. For e being and beyond, though, let me be satisfied with care. Amen.

Take Away: I take comfort in knowing God cares.

week 12

Melding Pot

Moving Toward a Blended Family

God sets the lonely in families.
Psalm 68:6

It may be that your days as a single mom are numbered, that yo
your fiancé are planning to blend a family. In your case, "his
"hers" will go beyond towels and cars to sons and daughters. B
pronoun is about to change, at least with regard to the kids.
child is about to become "yours" (in the singular as well as th
ral). If their other parent is still in the picture, your future hus
kids will have a dual identity—and hopefully loyalty. So will
if your ex is involved in their lives.

No one has promised that blending will be easy. The wor
(meaning blend) is a combination of *melt* and *weld*. Your bl
family will be like a melting pot. Some degree of merging wi
place naturally. But welding will require strenuous effort. Eac
involved is accustomed to fixed roles, based upon age, gende
order, your prior family constellation, and a variety of other f
The initial shakedown period will almost certainly be challeng

Conflicting advice from others will no doubt bombard yo

be your task to discern together which is wise and appropriate ur unique situation. Rely on the Word to help you decide. hock-full of invaluable helps, from kid- and-marriage-related bs to passages of incomparable hope, comfort, and promise. ally, inviting God as an equal partner in an already complicated will serve to smooth out the mix.

amily blending is on your near horizon, resolve to make every with the Spirit's guidance, to face the changes and challenges usly. If remarriage is your hope, continue to wait patiently for timing.

ther, you've graciously blended us, and every one of others and sisters in Christ, into your own forever y. We've joined our brother, your one and only Jesus, in a seamless union. Weld our combined es together, we pray, with the same strength and ency. Amen.

ke Away: My husband/fiancé and I rely on God's wisdom in blending our families.

week 12

Worry Equity

Waiting for Bumps in the Night

I will lie down and sleep in peace, for you alone,
O LORD, make me dwell in safety.
Psalm 4:8

As the responsible individual in the home, I anticipate bun the night. In fact, I've been known to lie awake in preparati California girl at heart, even though I've been a Michigande 1969, I have a healthy respect for cold (more like an inordina of freezing to death). In my mobile home my furnace pilot, to the roof, was susceptible to the slightest puff of wind. Or tery nights I'd catch myself lying awake, holding my breat the furnace once again kicked on. One night the hot-water in my bedroom closet sprang a leak. In subzero temperature outdoors on slippered feet to lie down in the snow, groping th insulation for the shutoff valve located two feet below the gro a protected hole.

Of course, nonmechanical emergencies can strike rando well—crises like sudden-onset flu, fire, burglary—you name it nights I sleep well. But there are those times when, for wh

, my taut nerves trigger a wake-up reflex.

couple of years ago I did fail to awaken to a 3 a.m. phone hristina called sheepishly from an ambulance, en route to the al following an auto accident, leaving a cryptic but reassuring ge on my answering machine. I did hear and respond to a call the emergency room at 4:20 the same morning. Khris was d and shaken but otherwise intact.

ghttime vigilance does little more than tire you out, making neffective to meet the demands that *will* from time to time your rest. Stored up worry equity does nothing to alleviate cumstances once a problem occurs, so why not let God do tching (he's already awake) and accept his gift of restorative

e kids are tucked in warmly, the deadbolts are l, the night lights are glowing, and my bedroom s halfway open, allowing me to keep one ear s I sleep. Allow me now, Night Watchman, to ith myself to the beckoning rest. Amen.

ke Away: God keeps watch while I sleep.

God's Arm

Flinging a Vertical Challenge

The LORD answered Moses, "Is the LORD's arm too sh
You will now see whether or not what I say
will come true for you."
Numbers 11:23

At five feet five I'm not exactly vertically challenged, although are moments when I'd appreciate the ability to extend my fing to latch on to a light bulb. My minor height limitation is no big But a problem ensues when I try to impose limitations on Go

In Numbers 11 Moses presented God with a vertical chal Irked by the people's insistence on adding meat to their diet vowed to gorge them on the stuff. Moses pointed out log problems God had evidently overlooked—to which the responded, presumably with some vehemence, "Is [my] ar short?"

If you're like me, you prefer to work out your own prol turning to prayer as a last resort. You may doubt God's in ability, or availability. You may be angry—even enrage him, ready to prove to him that you'll succeed no matte obstacles you envision him lobbing your way. You may elf on your resourcefulness. One way or another, though, attitude and actions fling a vertical challenge toward n.

lm 44 addresses God on the subject of the Israelites' conquest naan: "It was not by their sword that they won the land, nor eir arm bring them victory; it was your right hand, your . . *for you loved them*" (v. 3, emphasis added). Whatever the nstances that brought you to single motherhood, whatever onflicted emotions, don't doubt or disdain God's desire and to help you. He longs to embrace you and feel your arms ed around his neck in a return hug. He has your best interests t, every minute of every seemingly interminable day. Why? *e he loves you.*

ank you, God, that in your infinite love you ed down from on high and took hold of me." ace my family, I pray, in an eternal group hug. n.

ke Away: God's love and power see me through any and every circumstance.

Wrap It Up

Monday

Take Away

I bask in my Protector's undivided attention.

Tuck Away

When [Jesus] had finished washing their feet, he put on his cloth returned to his place. "Do you understand what I have done for yo asked them. (John 13:12)

Give Away

I'll bend my program to meet my friend's need. It won't brea neither will I!

Tuesday

Take Away

I take comfort in knowing God cares.

Tuck Away

I have loved you with an everlasting love; I have drawn you with kindness. (Jeremiah 31:3)

e Away

vite my neighbor into my circle of friendship—there within wider circle of caring.

dnesday

e Away

usband/fiancé and I rely on God's wisdom in blending our es.

: Away

r sons will be taught by the LORD, and great will be your children's In righteousness you will be established. (Isaiah 54:13–14)

Away

taken the step of a second marriage, complete with new chil- 'll share my insights and experiences with a friend who's poised into a similar initiation.

rsday

Away

eeps watch while I sleep.

Tuck Away

He who watches over you will not slumber. The sun will not harm ;
day, nor the moon by night. (Psalm 121:3, 6)

Give Away

I'll be on the alert for some opportunity to introduce my acq
tance to my Night Watchman.

Friday

Take Away

God's love and power see me through any and every circumsta

Tuck Away

To him who is able to keep you from falling and to present you bef
glorious presence without fault and with great joy—to the only G
Savior be glory, majesty, power and authority, through Jesus Chr
Lord, before all ages, now and forevermore! Amen. (Jude 24–25)

Give Away

I'll nudge my friend toward God's ever-expanding "inner"
God's embrace is wide enough to enfold one more.

notes

*Our greatest natural resource
is the minds of our children.*

Walt Disney

9 781416 58